The
Seven
Next
Words of Christ

The Seven Next Words of Christ

Finding Hope in the Resurrection Sayings

SHANE STANFORD

ABINGDON PRESS
NASHVILLE

THE SEVEN NEXT WORDS OF CHRIST
FINDING HOPE IN THE RESURRECTION SAYINGS

This book is printed on acid-free paper.

Library of Congress Cataloging-in-Publication Data

Stanford, Shane, 1970–
　The seven next words of Christ : finding hope in the Resurrection sayings / Shane Stanford.
　　p. cm.
　ISBN 0-687-49821-X (alk. paper)
　1. Jesus Christ—Words. 2. Jesus Christ—Resurrection. 3. Bible. N.T. Gospels—Criticism, interpretation, etc. 4. Bible. N.T. Acts—Criticism, interpretation, etc. I. Title.

BT306.S79 2006
232.9′7—dc22   2005029881

All scripture quotations unless noted otherwise are taken from the *New Revised Standard Version of the Bible*, copyright © 1989, by the Division of Christian Education of the National Council of the Churches of Christ in the United States of America. Used by permission. All rights reserved.

Scripture quotations noted Message are taken from *THE MESSAGE*. Copyright © Eugene Peterson, 1993, 1994, 1995. Used by permission of NavPress Publishing Group.

Scripture quotations noted NIV are taken from the HOLY BIBLE: NEW INTERNATIONAL VERSION®. Copyright © 1973, 1978, 1984 by the International Bible Society. Used by permission of Zondervan Publishing House. All rights reserved.

Scripture quotations noted NLT are taken from the Holy Bible, New Living Translation, copyright © 1996. Used by permission of Tyndale House Publishers, Inc., Wheaton, Illinois 60189. All rights reserved.

06 07 08 09 10 11 12 13 14 15—10 9 8 7 6 5 4 3 2 1

MANUFACTURED IN THE UNITED STATES OF AMERICA

In memory of
my grandfather Earl and my grandmother Dorothy,

for teaching me about the potential of
Grace to transform any situation.

Thank you for the example of a faithful journey.

In honor of
my grandmother Bettye,

for believing that my first book (circa second grade)
would certainly not be the last.

In anticipation for
Pokey, Sarai Grace, Juli Anna, and Emma Leigh,

for what God has in store.
I love you.

CONTENTS

INTRODUCTION

This project began more as an offhanded comment than as a book idea. The first time I truly considered the forty days following the Resurrection was during a Worship Design Team meeting at the church I founded and pastored for nearly nine years. Having developed our focus for the Lenten season, we turned our attention to the season following Easter. After the solemn display and reflection of Lent and the excitement of Easter morning, the weeks following Easter seem, at times, lost in the liturgical calendar. However, this is one of the most important times for congregations, especially in terms of attracting those who do not attend or at least marginally attend church. Many have made their way back to a local church during the Lenten experience only to find a loss of focus following Easter. I suggested to the congregation that, after the Resurrection, the work has only begun.

Therefore, while discussing ideas for post-Easter sermon series and themes, I casually mentioned that we should look at the "next words" or encounters of Jesus as possible suggestions. That particular year, the church offered a moving Good Friday service focusing on the familiar and traditional Seven Last Words of Christ. Could it be that there were similar encounters after the Resurrection?

To be quite honest, I thought I would discover various encounters with Jesus scattered in the post-Resurrection texts, offering repeated approaches to familiar scenes. Most pastors and theologians are aware of apparent differences in the Resurrection and post-Resurrection encounters, and an exact ordering of the chronology is difficult in sections. Thus, I approached the texts with skepticism as to what I would find and whether or not it would be helpful.

It didn't take long to realize that something amazing was happening. As the post-Resurrection encounters unfolded, I discovered they fit within particular categories. Some texts stood on their own, while others meshed with encounters in another Gospel. Also, the encounter in Acts 1 needed attention as a part of the overall scheme. True, some encounters are shrouded in debate as to the original intentions and time frame of the author. However, by the time I finished with my preliminary investigation, I realized that, much like the Seven Last Words on the Cross, there were seven primary, post-Resurrection themes. Each possessed a particular focus, and each, in unique ways, spoke an important truth for all believers.

Please understand, I do not write this as a New Testament scholar, but as a pastor and fellow sojourner of the faith. Although trained by some of the world's finest at Duke Divinity School, I approach the texts as narrative instead of as a historical or technical document. This book is not intended to be a Bible commentary, but a thematic interpretation of the continuing story of Jesus' amazing transformation of the world's spiritual landscape. Certainly, I realize that these seven *next words* of Jesus took nearly fifty years to compile, and the composition of each encounter deserves deep debate and instruction. But for my purpose, the Holy Spirit, in dramatic fashion, took what had begun as isolated texts in various Gospels, one intimate encounter or *word* after another, and bridged the span of nearly five decades. And, in similar fashion, the encounters did not remain isolated to these texts, but seemed to speak through the ages to our modern spiritual condition—almost coming to life as I read and studied. I concluded that, truly, God intended for these messages to reassure all believers, regardless of generation.

I also discovered that the themes of the *next words* seemingly correspond to the thematic narratives of the Seven Last Words of Christ. Although there is some debate as to the appropriate order of the Seven Last Words, for years I have used the order suggested by the *Book of Worship* of The United Methodist Church—accepted throughout most traditional circles. The Last Words came alive when read against the backdrop of Christ's post-Resurrection encounters. For instance, Jesus' first word on the cross is "Father, forgive them, for they know not what they do." Along with focusing on forgiveness, he focuses on people's lack of knowledge and understanding about his identity. The first *next word* after the Resurrection is also about Jesus' identity, when Jesus asks Mary the poignant question, "Who are you looking for?" As Jesus helps Mary see who is standing in front of her, her world is transformed, and she is more than aware of Jesus' presence in her midst. Another example is the final word on the cross: "Into thy hands I commit my spirit." As Jesus willingly gives up his spirit, God's redemption of the world is complete. The final *next word* of Christ, described in Acts 1, prepares for the coming of God's Spirit to earth as a means of helping the newly reconciled live redemptively in the world. Therefore, although a precise correlation is difficult to develop, the Last Words and *next words* correspond in the general tone of their message and purpose. It is as though God, through the hope of the *next words* of Christ, is answering the despair and struggle expressed in the Last Words of Jesus on the cross. If nothing else, I realized we should never underestimate the ability of the Holy Spirit to use the imprint of people and situations to record the infinite and continually unfolding work of God.

So what exactly are the *seven next words* of Jesus? Like the Seven Last Words, these words or conversations provide insight into the heart and mind of Jesus as he encouraged, prepared, and deployed his disciples for ministry to the world. Building to a crescendo with the Ascension in Acts 1 (the *seventh next word*), Jesus surprises, consoles, rebukes, and ignites the actions and passions of his followers through seven powerful encounters. These moments lead us through emotional highs and lows, helping us explore our own frailties and possibilities along the way.

The *seven next words* are taken from the post-Resurrection texts of the four Gospels and the book of Acts. Again, some of the encounters are duplications from one text to another. Surprisingly (or not), despite some retelling of the same story, seven unique interactions with Jesus personally connect the reader to Christ's care, compassion, and purpose for his believers.

Like the Seven Last Words of Christ, the *seven next words* are arranged chronologically, based on the particular encounter with Jesus and the theme involved. They do not represent the order in which the Gospels were written. The style of the book is more narrative than instructional, building on a point-and-parable model rather than on outline form. The stories and illustrations drawn from modern life are based on actual situations, but the names and circumstances of the people involved have been changed to conceal their identities. Although anyone will enjoy the work, the primary audience is those searching for a deeper connection or reconnection to Christ.

I hope each of us will see the unveiling of God's grace and forgiveness as we examine these encounters together. I want Jesus' words to ignite in believers and seekers alike our need for true relationship with God and the peace that comes from knowing, walking, and talking with Christ. To this end, I have used various translations of Scripture, from the New Revised Standard Version to the New Living Bible to Petersen's *Message*. My purpose is to provide the clearest and most meaningful account of Jesus' words and the situations that surround them. However, I also encourage readers to immerse themselves fully in the language and text so that they can experience personally the subtle nuances of Scripture. For while I believe in the divine imprint of the Scriptures, I also believe that God and God's word are greater than what can be found on any written page. The story of God's love through Jesus transcends any language or culture. Thus, the real story of Scripture is that it is our story too.

On that note, let me say that the book contains several stories from my own journey as a hemophiliac and as a person living with HIV. I share these stories because of the personal way these encounters have shaped my understanding of faith and have comforted me along the journey. I learned *several miles ago* that I cannot separate my love of Jesus from personal experiences. Actually, I believe no one can. To that end, please bear with me.

As you read this book, I pray that God will open your eyes and your mind to the story of Jesus, so that you can see the living presence of Scripture even today. The characters and settings will be familiar to each of us. Peter's hubris, Thomas's doubts, and Mary Magdalene's devotion unveil personal stories that will be recognized by both today's person of faith and the skeptic. I pray that you will not miss the peripheral characters, those who sit by the city gates and walk quietly behind the scenes, reminding us of our own modern-day marginalized and forgotten. I pray that as we study the texts together, you will hear the echo of the unwritten word, cry, or chuckle that brings these stories to life—possibly even catching a glimpse of yourself in the process. But, more than anything else, I pray God will open your heart to see the impressive and powerful nature of the gospel in our midst—to know the Jesus of these pages as the Lord of your life and as your dearest friend. May God bless you.

Last Words First

Die in a Decent Manner

No one was more American, or more human for that matter, than Benjamin Franklin. Brilliant but eccentric, crude but possessing exquisite taste and manners, personable but deeply reflective, cynical but overtly religious, he is a subject at once of both great enlightenment and confusion. Benjamin Franklin's intuition about subjects ranging from science to government to human rights makes him possibly the most accomplished and important of the founders of this country. Even one of his most vocal critics, John Adams, could not help admitting that "Franklin had a genius, original, sagacious and inventive, capable of discoveries in science no less than improvement in the fine arts and the mechanical arts. He had a vast imagination" (Walter Isaacson, *Benjamin Franklin: An American Life* [New York: Simon & Schuster, 2003], 477). Remarkably, most of the accomplishments with which we today are familiar happened after his sixtieth birthday. For many of his contemporaries, he seemed almost immortal. But Franklin was quite aware of his mortality. During the last years of his life, he wrote that his marble tombstone should be "six feet long, four feet wide, plain, with only a small molding rounding the upper edge, and this inscription: Benjamin and Deborah Franklin" (Isaacson, *Benjamin Franklin*, 470).

As with our own loved ones, his family and friends were particularly resistant to the idea of Franklin's eventual passing. They could not bear the thought of such a great man being removed from their presence. Even as death was drawing close, Franklin, very sick from pulmonary problems, roused himself long enough to request that his bed be properly made so that he could "die in a decent manner." His daughter, Sally, seeing one last rise from the old gentleman, remarked to Franklin that he might be recovering. To her surprise, Franklin calmly replied, "I hope not" (Isaacson, *Benjamin Franklin*, 469). These would be his last words.

As large, colorful, and talented as Franklin was, even he could not postpone the inevitable. For Franklin, as for all of us, last words truly are final. But there lived one whose last words were not final—in fact, they were merely a prologue to a larger, more glorious text whose opening words are the subject of this book.

A Place Called Calvary

The sky darkened, and a strange hue formed over the horizon. Although it was only noon, it seems as though life itself was being lost. As the cross was lifted into place, those in the crowd could believe what they saw—such a good man, such a good friend being tortured and, now, being killed. The mourners, the spectators, those drunk with the smell of death, Jesus' mother letting out a muffled cry—it was almost more than any decent human being could endure.

Maybe that is why Jesus' *first word* shakes them so: "Father, forgive them; for they do not know what they are doing" (Luke 23:34). After everything, including the beating, the mockery of a trial, and during the crucifixion, he asked for his executioners to be forgiven? At this point, forgiveness and justice seemed two concepts very far apart.

For the next moments, there were no other sounds—only the groans and desperate pleas of the two men hanging beside Jesus. Then the insults began—the guards, the leaders, even one of the criminals. But while the first criminal mocked him, shouting insults about saving the three of them, the other criminal finally said, "Do you not fear God, since you are under the same sentence of condemnation? And we indeed have been condemned justly, for we are getting what we deserve for our deeds, but this man has done nothing wrong." Then the criminal turned to Jesus: "Remember me when you come into your kingdom" (Luke 23:40-42). Jesus lifted his head toward his defender and said, "Truly I tell you, today you will be with me in Paradise" (Luke 23:43).

From the beginning of these horrible hours, from the trial to his death at Golgotha, Mary, Jesus' mother, never left his side. Everyone knew that

Jesus was close to his mother. Their relationship of love and great care was evident. They had experienced the traditional mother-son conversations, and at times Jesus proceeded down paths of which Mary did not approve. But, especially in these final moments, no one doubted their love for each other. That is why when Jesus lifted his head to speak to her, for any parent or child, the scene became nearly unbearable. He nodded toward John and said, "Woman, here is your son." Then, looking at John, he adds, "Here is your mother" (John 19:26*b*, 27*a*). It is remarkable that, given all that was taking place, Jesus stopped to make sure that his mother was cared for. For many, it seems odd that Jesus would be worried about such matters, but for those who knew him, it made all the sense in the world. This interaction also validated the distinctly intimate way they had experienced this remarkable man. The miracles had amazed them, but it was these deeply personal, human moments that connected them to him.

As the hours moved on, Jesus raised his head, but instead of addressing someone around the cross, his voice trailed upward. The scream is startling: "My God, my God, why have you forsaken me?" (Matthew 27:46). For a man of such faith, the words seemed out of place. Some thought he was calling Elijah, but for those who journeyed with him and now stood at a distance, the words seemed almost palpable, and they were clearly addressed to God. What sadness his disciples must have felt—first, for their dying teacher and friend, but also because they had never witnessed anyone so alone.

Then, almost as a concession, Jesus looked to the guards standing at the foot of the cross and said, "I am thirsty" (John 19:28). Though many failed to understand what this meant, Jesus knew, and as the syllables rolled from his mouth, the words of the psalmist were fulfilled: "My strength has dried up like sunbaked clay. My tongue sticks to the roof of my mouth. You have laid me in the dust and left me for dead" (Psalm 22:15 NLT). After everything, Jesus had nothing left to give.

Finally Jesus raised his head one last time and said, "It is finished" (John 19:30). "Into your hands, I commend my Spirit" (Luke 23:46). For what seemed an eternity, the world shook. Rocks fell, all the guards but one vanished, and the sightseers ran for cover. When the excitement subsided, only the women remained, standing firmly but distant from the cross. Rumors abound about these last, unbelievable moments. Some say the veil in the temple tore at the exact moment Jesus died; others claim that the dead were raised. Regardless, something remarkable happened. Crucifixion is supposed to take longer, most times ending with the breaking of the criminal's legs. But that did not happen with Jesus. In one final miracle, he simply allowed himself to die. In the chaos that followed, most did not even realize what they had seen, except for one Roman soldier, who looked to the cross and uttered, "Truly this man was God's Son!" (Matthew 27:54). Ironically, after three years of ministry, preaching, miracles, and change, at the end it was one Gentile who truly understood.

Soon, it was time to take him down. The burial would require assistance, but after all the confusion and fear of the past twenty-four hours, who would dare help? Mary, Jesus' mother, thought, *He came into the world without a place to lay his head; now, in his death, we have no place to lay his body.* But someone had seen Joseph of Arimathea, and he promised to assist them. A Pharisee no less, he recoiled in horror at the past hours, ashamed and distraught at all that had happened.

For the disciples, their next steps are uncertain. Their world shattered, their hearts aching, they wondered, *Why go on at all?* But their faith gave them an inner strength, and they knew life must continue. Besides, Jesus would have expected no less. Whatever it took, they must make sure they cared for Jesus, for that is exactly what he had done for them. Still, the echo of his last words rang within them: "It is finished."

How could they have known that actually it had just begun?

THE FIRST WORD

Who are you looking for?

John 20:1-18

Department Store Counseling

"Can I help you find what you are looking for?" I said to the short, middle-aged lady standing next to me in the aisle at a local department store. I had no idea how that question would affect my day.

"I can't reach that box!" she said, glaring at a large container of assorted tissues. "I called for help several minutes ago, but no one around here seems to care." The tone of her voice suggested the issue of gaining someone's attention was much more complex than simply acquiring a box of tissues. "It's been like this all morning," she said, her voice now quivering a bit. "I can't get anyone to listen or care about what I am saying." The tears began to well up in her eyes. At that moment, the realization of how and what she was saying hit her, and she quickly turned away attempting to find—of all things—a tissue.

"Would you like to talk about it?" I asked, knowing full well that I really didn't mean it but, given the situation, felt obliged to offer. I introduced myself and said that I pastored the United Methodist church down the street. She made a few obligatory nice remarks about the church, and then, to my surprise, agreed that talking might help. Having been up most of the previous night, I was tired and a little irritable. The thought of having to counsel someone in a department store on a Saturday morning did not enthrall me; the thought of doing so while standing up was even less appealing. Asking the lady to wait for a moment, I searched for a place to sit down. I found it two aisles over, in the home and garden section. Sitting on the second shelf was a stack of plastic deck chairs. I removed two chairs from the shelf, placed them at the end of the row, and encouraged the lady to sit and talk.

At first she was noticeably apprehensive. Like me, she was experiencing what was undoubtedly her first department store counseling session. However, after a few moments of discomfort, she opened up. She told me about a marriage that was unraveling, dysfunctional children, and a life that seemed out of control. I am not sure how long we talked, but I remember, after praying with her and giving her my business card, that she looked at me and said, "I guess sometimes God helps us find things we don't even know we are looking for." As we parted company, it struck me that she never got her box of tissues.

Mary's Encounter

I can imagine Mary Magdalene's surprise that Easter morning when she arrived at an empty tomb. The weekend must have been torture. For several years she had followed Jesus, tending to his needs as well as to those of the disciples. Her commitment must have raised more than one set of eyebrows, but that did not hinder her dedication to Jesus' ministry. She had been there for everything: the miracles, the confrontations, the exhilaration. She had watched as they led him back and forth from the priests to Herod to Pilate. A horrified Mary Magdalene saw the disdain with which they treated him, and I am sure she cringed with every blow of the soldiers' whips. She made the trek to Calvary, heard Jesus' last words, watched him die, and helped lay him in the tomb. Her arrival on Sunday morning was not simply to tend to the Messiah; it was to care for the body of a friend.

She panicked when she found the empty tomb. Running to the only people she could trust, she told Peter and John. After seeing for themselves, they left, wondering what might happen next. The passage gives no indication that either Peter or John talked with Mary about what they had seen. Consumed with what they had just witnessed, they left her standing alone at the tomb. She stood motionless, watching, but did not leave. Finally, after what must have seemed an eternity, she lowered her face to the tomb and peered inside. There she saw two men.

"Why are you crying?" one asked. She replied, "They have taken my Lord." Then she heard the question again, but this time it came from behind her. Turning around, she encountered a third man. He seemed familiar, but, especially at this moment, she couldn't place him. *Maybe he is the gardener,* she thinks. The third man asked, "Who are you looking for?" Politely, humbly, she stepped forward. "Sir," she said, "if you have taken him away, tell me where you have put him, and I will go and get him."

The man looked her in the eyes and replied, "Mary." She wasn't sure she heard him correctly. But as the echo of her name faded, she gazed at him and found the one for whom she was looking.

Mary's encounter with Jesus resonates with all of us. At some time or other we have all watched helplessly as our lives spin out of control, as the meaning slowly seeps away, leaving us with no direction or destination. We go through the motions, taking care of obligations, but gone are the passion and the purpose behind it all. Of all the post-Resurrection encounters, Mary's is the most personal. It speaks not to our theological understandings, our evangelical responsibilities, or even our deepest faith. This encounter speaks to our hearts. Mary may very well have been the person closest to Jesus. Her faith did not waiver; she remained through thick and thin; but even Mary, on this day, stood before the risen Savior and mistook him for the gardener.

For many of us, mistaking Jesus for the gardener is the least of our problems. The pace of our hectic lives not only leaves us unable to see the work of God around us, but keeps us from realizing our need for God in the first place. Stumbling through Christ's presence at the tomb means little to those of us who never made the journey at all. It is not that we can't find who we are looking for; rather, like my friend from the department store, we aren't even aware that someone is missing.

Hearing Him Call My Name

Bill understood this struggle better than anyone I had ever known. A successful engineer, he had the right degrees, a beautiful wife, three talented children, and a gorgeous home. For years, Bill and his family lived behind a facade of contentment and accomplishment. However, the inner workings of Bill's life were in shambles. Although he did not fully comprehend the severity of the situation, Bill's marriage had begun to crumble years earlier. His aloof behavior and cold demeanor drained the relationship of its life. Bill's children, although rich in possessions, lacked the one thing they desperately wanted and needed: his affection and affirmation.

Bill's understanding of faith was cynical at best. Although he grew up in a Christian home, Bill attended church more out of obligation than belief. By the time he finished college, he considered church a crutch for emotional and intellectual cripples and relied on logic, intellect, and talent to make his way in the world.

I met Bill through his wife. A member of a sister congregation I served in North Carolina, Jan was a delightful, committed Christian who cared deeply about her family, her faith, and the church. Her one desire was that her family be healed and that her husband's heart find peace. Bill not only recoiled against Jan's faith, he purposefully taunted her commitment to the church.

Jan called on a Monday to inform me that she was leaving Bill and returning home to South Carolina. Although this was a decision that she had made in her mind several times, this was the first time she had mustered the courage to follow through. The divorce was painful to watch. Jan had given more than twenty-five years of her life to a failed marriage and to a person who, to many of us, seemed a lost soul. The only redeeming feature of the whole episode was Jan's release from struggle as she finally let go of the relationship. Among her final words before she left town was the desire that Bill might one day calm the storm that was destroying him.

After Jan left, rumors spread through town that Bill was not doing well. In spite of the rumors, when I ran into him at a local restaurant, his emotional and physical condition shocked me. Gone was the bravado, and he had lost nearly thirty pounds. His eyes looked as if he had been crying. We exchanged pleasantries, and then, near the end of the conversation, I told him to give me a call if he ever wanted to talk. Several days later, he did call.

Bill accepted Christ in my office and began what remains one of the most powerful journeys of restoration I have ever seen. Over the next two years, Bill stooped and peeked inside the empty tomb of his life. It was painful and, at times, wrenching. But he did not waiver, believing that this might be the only way to heal his broken life. Bill wrestled with old demons, past lies, and hollow assumptions that had led him far from faith.

Nearly two years after Bill arrived in my office, he gave his testimony to his local church. I had left town by that time, but I received a tape of the service. He spoke eloquently about grace, about God's unfailing love, and about enough forgiveness "to save even him." I scribbled his closing words on the back of a Sunday bulletin: "I never realized I was lost or that I, of all people, needed to be found. . . . But they kept talking about grace, and I knew that God was speaking to me."

Two years ago Bill was remarried to a wonderful Christian woman. He remains a committed leader in his church and a powerful witness to God's grace. Bill also exemplifies the sweetness of recognizing the Master's voice and of hearing him call your name.

Why Are You Crying?

Have you ever wondered why Jesus felt the need to repeat this question? Undoubtedly, he had been standing behind Mary long enough to hear her explanation to the angels. She had repeated to them the same plea she gave to Peter and John, "They have taken away my Lord, and I do not know where they have laid him" (John 20:13). But no one seemed to care. Mary's grief was evident. When she turned to hear the third man repeat the question, her frustration with the situation grew. Why did Jesus ask again?

Although known for his compassion and patience, Jesus could also probe deep into a person's soul when wanting to make a point or elicit a reaction. Jesus' followers had seen this tactic before—Jesus watching patiently for the right opportunity to insert a question or statement that might prick the scab on a person's soul and begin, unbeknownst to the person, the process of real healing.

One of the more memorable episodes occurred when two sisters began to argue over what one considered the other's lack of attention to task. On this particular occasion, Jesus had come to the home of Lazarus, Martha, and Mary to enjoy the company of his followers. Sometime during the visit, Martha accused her sister Mary of neglecting the guests. Mary had been sitting at the feet of Jesus, listening to his message instead of assisting Martha in the kitchen.

Martha pleaded with Jesus to scold Mary or, at the very least, tell her to help. Jesus responded not by addressing Mary, but by speaking to Martha. With a soft, unaccusing tone, Jesus told Martha that Mary had chosen "the better part." It was a direct, if not deriding, way of showing Martha that her attention to the details of the day, although important, were not the primary need for Mary. Mary did not need to attend to any detail but that of her own soul (Luke 10:38-42). The same can be said of Mary Magdalene standing at the tomb. While consumed with the details, she missed the blessing. And so, to shake her from the burden of her tasks, Jesus asked the question again.

Cecilia

Cecilia's life reeked of past mistakes and failures. Once a dutiful wife, she now lived mostly from street corner to street corner, finding solace in drugs and illicit sex. To comprehend the journey that brought her here seems impossible. One bad choice led to a dozen others, and this mother of five lost everything. Her third child, Michael, was a dedicated investment banker whose life seemingly could not be more different from that of his mother. He was tall and strong, a combination of actor and accomplished athlete. He had long, wavy hair through which he continually ran his fingers, a habit he could neither explain nor curtail. He was a doting father and husband, and his favorite moments were singing his children to sleep. Michael's life suggested a perfect home, one with the quintessential mother, father, dog, and cat. Nothing could have been further from the truth.

Michael first shared the details of his upbringing while attending a morning prayer group. His calm, subdued manner quickly changed when he began talking about his parents. His older siblings were able to escape before the bottom fell out. But Michael, the oldest of the second group of children, experienced it all. His parents fought often, and Michael served as the protector of his younger brother and sister. His mother's struggles increased when she began an improper relationship, the result largely of a husband who worked too much and cared too little. Seeking comfort and affirmation, she became involved with a neighbor. This liaison was the first of many.

After several months of the same pattern, Michael's father divorced his mother, gained custody of the children, and moved away. Michael's infrequent contact with his mother further strained the relationship. Michael's father, unable to reconcile his own emotions, drank heavily. The physical abuse began a year after the divorce. For two years following that, Michael and his siblings slept under their beds, afraid of what their father might do.

Michael said the gunshot woke him around 1:30 A.M. Tiptoeing into the kitchen, he saw that the door to the garage was open. Peering around the corner, Michael viewed his father's body lying facedown near the back of the car. Moving quickly to ensure that his siblings would not see the body, Michael ushered them to a back bedroom and called the police.

The authorities were unable to locate their mother, and so Michael and his brother and sister were sent to Arkansas to live with their older sister. He found life at his sister's house awkward, as she and her new husband started their own family. Michael's primary goal was to make sure that his younger siblings were all right. At fifteen, he became their surrogate father and mother, the link to what could have been. Michael explained that those experiences made him determined to create a better home and a life that would mean something. So, mature and incredibly focused, Michael pressed toward the future, vowing never to look around the corners of his past again.

It is against this backdrop that a prayer partner first asked Michael, "Have you seen your mother lately?" Michael curtly and abruptly answered no. Three weeks later, another prayer partner asked the same question, again to a quick and absolute negative. The question kept coming, and one day Michael's eyes welled up with tears. "Please don't ask me that anymore," he said, attempting to be respectful. "I don't want to know where she is." The truth was that he did want to know, and that scared him more than anything else. That tomb had long been sealed, and the hovering demons were just too overwhelming.

The emotional battle reached a fever pitch when, after much prodding from his prayer group and with the help of two private investigators,

Michael discovered his mother living in a crime-ridden section of Jackson, Mississippi. The investigator indicated that she migrated from one crack house to another within a particular three-block radius. Cecilia has become a poignant example of a battered soul running for her life and, literally, going nowhere. The picture was traumatic and pathetic. Cecilia used her body to obtain drugs, oftentimes being left horribly abused when the "client" refused to pay.

The house where Michael finally found her was the last in a series of addresses given to him by the investigator. When he opened the door, the stench nearly knocked him off his feet. Of all of the ways the investigator attempted to prepare Michael for what he might find, he had not mentioned the intense and unique odor of a drug house. Gathering his bearings, Michael proceeded through a small entryway into what appeared to be a makeshift laboratory. A voice from behind the sofa startled him.

"Who are you?" asked a half-dressed man sitting slumped in a beanbag chair, obviously high as he stared blankly into a snowy television picture.

"I'm looking for someone," Michael said firmly, trying to appear calmer and stronger than he felt.

"Who are you looking for?" the man asked, never taking his eyes off the screen.

"Cecilia," Michael replied.

The man turned toward Michael and with a sly laugh asked, "What would you possibly want with that old whore?"

Ignoring the response, Michael asked again, this time more firmly, "Do you know where she is?"

"She's out back," said the man, and, with that, he turned back toward the television.

Michael found his mother lying naked on a rusty cot just inside a dingy, infested shack. A tourniquet was still on her arm; a needle rested on the floor, half visible under the bed. She was alive but unconscious. Looking around for something to cover her body, Michael wrapped his mother in a piece of black tarp. Carefully, he lifted Cecilia from the floor and cradled her in his arms. For three blocks in the brisk night air Michael carried his mother, unaware that each step represented a journey of redemption.

Cecilia spent six months in a chemical dependency facility in south Mississippi. Hundreds of hours of therapy and group discussion provided less healing than the one-hour visits Michael spent with his mother each week. During those six months, Michael was introduced to a woman in her mid-fifties who was shy but quite intelligent. She liked art but read the Sunday comics first. This woman, found naked in a shack, once owned an impressive collection of exquisitely dressed porcelain dolls. Baseball was her favorite sport, Jimmy Stewart her favorite actor, and ice cream her favorite food. Her sweetest childhood memory was sitting under the night sky with her father counting the stars. But, amidst the hours of discussion, Cecilia revealed that the most peaceful times of her life were the stolen moments late at night, when she walked into the bedroom of her middle child, sang him lullabies, and gently caressed his thick blond hair.

Jesus asked Mary the question again because deep down we all know the reason, and names, for our tears. . . .

Acclaimed theologian Henri J. M. Nouwen states in his work *Reaching Out* that "we do not have to deny or avoid our loneliness, our hostilities and illusions. To the contrary: When we have the courage to let these realities come to our full attention, understand them and confess them, then they slowly can be converted into solitude, hospitality and prayer" ([New York: Phoenix Press, 1985], 161). Jesus' questions forced Mary to encounter herself—her fears, desires, and possibilities, the pinnacles of her soul's potential. We should never forget that no one understood the principle of dying to self in order to be raised to newness of life better than did Jesus.

You Are Part of the Family

The chorus of the passage is found in Jesus' instructions for Mary: "Go and tell the disciples that I have not yet returned to my Father and *your Father*, to my God and *your God*." Jesus' intentions in these remarks rest not in the detail, but in the implications: "Go, Mary," Jesus entreats. "Tell them that you have seen me, but also tell them that we are family." For a bunch of malcontents who had left him at the cross, these are cherished words. But they are also words that Mary needed to hear. Someone does care, someone does listen, and that someone is no less than God.

Dear friend, this story belongs to us. Each of us, in one way or another, can identify with John, Peter, or Mary. Some are John, running ahead to the tomb, excited by the possibilities but anxious about entering. Others are Peter, hanging back, wondering what will be worse—finding him dead or alive. If he is dead, then our hopes are shattered; if he is alive, then we are forced to confront our shame. In either case, we need to know. But many are Mary, finding life has not turned out as expected, for whom the weight of the world has become overwhelming. But, no matter with whom we identify, what we find at the tomb is the same—hope and a risen Christ.

Millennia have passed, but the questions have not changed: Why are you crying? Who are you looking for? Jesus remains at the tombs of our lives, in the dark corners of our past, begging us to look inside and see the power of a new beginning. My prayer for each of us is that we will not allow the weight of our uncertainties to keep us from seeing the risen Jesus.

THE SECOND WORD

Greetings…Don't be afraid

Matthew 28:8-10

He is going ahead of you to Galilee. You will see him there." The words played a thousand times in their minds as the women ran to tell the disciples. One of the women, Mary Magdalene, kept telling herself again and again, *It was an angel! It was an angel!* It couldn't have been anything else. The white robe, the light! She had never seen anything more beautiful and yet more frightening, more peaceful and yet so shocking.

Maybe it was the rush of things changing so quickly. Only moments before, Mary Magdalene and the other Mary had arrived at the tomb prepared to care for a dead body. Now, they were running to tell the disciples about what had happened. It didn't necessarily make sense, but it also felt more *right* than anything they had ever experienced.

They heard his greeting first. The voice was unmistakable, but could it be? The two women slowed, dazed and confused by what they had just heard. Then, they both must have seen the same figure. Moving from the corner of their vision came a familiar face. They stopped and immediately fell to the ground. Neither spoke. Each of them grabbed at the man's feet, holding on as a drowning person grasps for life. Once again, the sound of the man's voice echoed what their eyes had seen but their hearts were hesitant to confirm.

Don't be afraid. For just a moment, as though time were standing still, they remembered the stories when he had uttered these words before. It was at a wedding in Cana during which a wine shortage would have ruined the most important event in a young couple's life. It was in the dusty marketplace as he lifted a woman from the dirt of despair and transformed her life forever. It was at a tomb where a friend and follower made his way to life again. It was when Jesus walked on the water and calmed a sudden storm. It was on the occasion of his arrest in what had been a tranquil garden. These were not hollow words; time and again, they changed everything.

Frank and Margaret

Everyone said that Frank and Margaret held the world on a string. Now, sitting in a hospital room, they couldn't believe what they were hearing. *Brain tumor? Malignant? How could this be?* The doctors said Margaret had a rare and aggressive type of tumor that was nearly always fatal. Certain experimental treatments might extend Margaret's life, but none had been notably successful in staving off the tumor's debilitating and eventually terminal effects. The doctors concluded that Margaret had perhaps six months to live. *Six months?* Frank's questions for the doctors were punctuated by moments of wrenching silence and quiet sobs. Margaret stared blankly at the wall. *World on a string*, she thinks. The string began to unravel, and their world was spinning out of control.

They met while undergrads. When people asked if they were dating, they responded with a sheepish grin, "No, we are just friends." But everyone knew they were much more. Neither could imagine life without the other. Both were accepted to Yale Law School, and a year later they were married in a simple ceremony at a small chapel just outside Wilmington, Delaware. Having no money for a formal honeymoon, Frank and Margaret spent their first night as a married couple in a small, rundown country inn named Becky's Bridal Barn. (Breakfast was free!) The honeymoon had to wait until school and jobs allowed it. There would be plenty of time for such things.

Following law school, they were hired by the same firm—Frank specialized in tax law while Margaret practiced in the exciting world of corporate mergers and buyouts. Everything came very quickly—the money, cars, and trips abroad, but also the problems that oftentimes disrupt the most solid of marriages. Eventually, with their paths barely crossing and their dreams proceeding in opposite directions, Frank and Margaret found themselves merely enduring their life together. And yet quiet moments, usually while they were thousands of miles apart, provided glimpses of emotion or feeling that reminded them of happier days. However, these moments passed quickly. Now, after fourteen years of what had seemed to outsiders like the perfect marriage, their relationship was marked by a deep sadness about what could have been. They were millionaires, and yet they had not even found time to take that honeymoon.

At first Margaret thought the headaches were due to stress or poor nutrition. But, over the past weeks, their severity increased and she noticed a slight change in her vision. Then, while giving a lecture in Washington, D.C., she became nauseated and blacked out. She hesitated to call Frank, who had been engulfed in major litigation concerning one of the firm's most important clients. However, the hospital called him, and, much to Margaret's surprise, Frank drove immediately to D.C.

Now, in the hospital room, Frank said softly, "We will get through this." Margaret looked at him. She didn't know what to say. As the tears streamed down her cheeks, Frank got up and put his arms around her. It was the first time in years that she could remember him really holding her. This was when it all broke free, and the rush of emotion overtook her. For the next hour Frank held her as she cried.

Over the weeks that followed, Margaret endured a series of difficult tests and treatments. She lost her hair, and her complexion became splotchy from the various medicines. But Frank, always at her side, left her small notes of encouragement, even if they were written in the language of a tax lawyer. The notes never failed to make her smile, and smiles were a rare commodity in her daily routine. Frank even took a sabbatical from work, and, to Margaret's delight, sold their penthouse and bought a home forty-five miles from the city.

When it became obvious that the treatments were no longer productive, Frank and Margaret stopped them and prepared for the end. Meetings, cross-country trips, and high-profile lunches were set aside for long walks and conversation. Margaret still had good days, and they made the most of them. They held hands, caught each other staring during stolen moments, and found love notes placed throughout the house. Although it was a time of great anxiety and stress, it seemed, to both of them, in an almost surreal way, to be unbelievably good. The future had never been so uncertain, and yet, for Frank and Margaret, their love for each other could not have been stronger. Surrounded by death, they found hope.

Margaret's thirty-eighth birthday marked the nine-month anniversary of her diagnosis. She had outlived the doctors' predictions by three months. However, the tumor was growing. Her vision deteriorated and her equilibrium was easily upset. Thankfully, there were no signs of dementia or other cognitive disruptions. Still, Margaret's decline was noticeable, especially to friends and colleagues. Although Frank and Margaret knew that time was not in their favor, they continued to make the most of each moment.

Unable to plan the honeymoon of their dreams because of Margaret's health, Frank instead arranged to rent an entire bed-and-breakfast for two weeks in a lovely village just off Chesapeake Bay. It had been years since they had been to that part of the country. Their first night at the inn, as they watched the sunset, they realized they were just an hour's drive from their wedding chapel and, more important, from Becky's Bridal Barn. They laughed as they considered how far away those places were, in circumstances if not miles. This most unassuming of honeymoons had been one of the happiest times in their lives. Neither realized it, but it had been the Becky's Bridal Barn moments of their lives that had kept them together, when logic told them to give up.

For two weeks there was one beautiful sunset after another. Frank, not ordinarily a religious person, felt there was something almost supernatural about the sunsets, as though a higher being was setting a stage for two people in love. For the first time in his life, Frank began to think that maybe this world was not an accident.

Two days before they were scheduled to leave, Margaret had a setback. She awoke unable to move her left arm. The feeling gradually returned, but by nightfall she was exhausted from the day's frustrations and from her painkillers and other medications. Frank continued with plans and served a seven-course meal, even though Margaret was able to eat very little.

After dinner, as they watched another beautiful sunset, Margaret brought up the topic both of them had been avoiding all day. "Frank," she began softly, "you know this will not have a happy ending."

For a moment Frank sat quietly, continuing to watch the sunset. Finally he said, "Sweetheart, I know that. But, instead of happy endings, I have learned something more important. I have learned to celebrate the here and now." With that, Margaret laid her head on his shoulder, and they quietly watched as the curtain closed on another day.

The coroner reported that Margaret died sometime during the night, apparently of a stroke. She felt no pain, and by all accounts her death was peaceful. Frank called the authorities around 6 A.M. Surprisingly, it had been one of the most peaceful night's sleep he had experienced in months. They went to bed fully dressed, with Margaret lying on his left arm and holding his right hand in hers. The last sound Frank heard from Margaret was a gentle sigh sometime during the night.

The funeral service was beautiful but simple. Friends from all over the country made their way to pay respects to one of the brightest and toughest legal minds in the field. Frank couldn't help smiling as people described Margaret's tenacious, go-after-it-at-all-costs attitude. He had certainly seen a different side over the past few months. Much to the surprise of family and close friends, Frank chose a small cemetery in Delaware for Margaret's interment. To many, its choice was difficult to fathom. The headstones were unspectacular and the grounds in desperate need of repair. Most disturbing was the god-awful neon sign flashing from across the street, whose only remaining readable words were *Becky* and *barn*.

To Frank the attorney, the previous nine months did not make sense. The rapid sequence of events overwhelmed even his superb mind, which was trained to assimilate facts and logic. But to Frank the man and the husband, the previous nine months represented a redemption of sorts. Even in the loss of his wife, Frank found his best friend again, and a relationship that seemed dead was resurrected even as her body faded. What he lost in this world, Frank realized, he had found in his soul. In fact, Margaret and he said it many times: if this was what it took to bring them back together, then it was worth it, for the sweetness far outweighed the pain.

Frank visited Margaret's grave often over the following years. Each time, he brought two things—a cup full of sand (taken from shores of the Chesapeake) and a rose. And he could not help smiling as he read the epitaph: *And they lived happily ever after . . . every day!*

Unexpected Paths

I first heard the story of Frank and Margaret while attending a conference on HIV/AIDS issues. I spoke in the morning about opportunities for communities to be involved in HIV/AIDS ministries and led a workshop later in the day. At lunch, one of my tablemates introduced himself and commented on my presentation. As we talked, I was fascinated by the gentleman's keen sense of mission and depth of purpose. He had worked for several years as legal counsel for a hospice consortium in Washington, D.C. He was attending the conference as a presenter on liability issues facing nonprofits over the next decade.

What sparked our conversation was a passage of scripture I used at the close of my presentation:

> Trust in the LORD with all your heart,
>   and do not rely on your own insight.
> In all your ways acknowledge him,
>   and he will make straight your paths.
>
> (Proverbs 3:5-6)

The gentleman introduced himself simply as Frank, and our conversation ensued from there. He mentioned growing up Catholic although he was never very active in his local parish. In fact, he did not become interested in religion until a few years before, following the death of his wife, Margaret. He continued, saying, "At her funeral, the priest read from Proverbs 3. I would have never thought much about the words, but, during Margaret's illness, I began, well, talking to God." Frank paused for a moment. "It wasn't really praying. It was talking...like you and I are talking."

Frank continues, "All of us crave that connection, and in the absence of it we will fill the void with anything—but we are never satisfied. I could never figure out why, even with Margaret so very sick, the more I read, prayed, and watched the miracle of everyday life, the less afraid I was of the future. Then, it hit me: the real discontent of human existence is not fear; it is spiritual hunger—the desire for making sense of it all, and the hope that, in some way or another, it matters."

I thought to myself, *Could it really be so simple? Was this the real key to the good news?* Perhaps God came, not to take away our fears, but to alleviate this all-consuming hunger. If this is true, the nature of the Resurrection, and of the entire Christian life for that matter, is not one of perseverance, but of feasting on the promise of God's unfolding work of grace. In this light, Paul's words in Romans 8 seem all the more pertinent: "What then are we to say about these things? If God is for us, who is against us?" (v. 31).

Refilled for the Journey

Once I arrived home from the conference, I spent time looking at Jesus' own words concerning fear. I discovered that on nineteen occasions Jesus told his followers to be unafraid. But the context for each was different. Some statements related to personal conditions such as illness and persecution. Others dealt with relational problems. Still others described uncertainty about the future. However, in each circumstance Jesus' request for his followers to be unafraid paralleled his plea for the listener to refocus on God. As Frank said in our conversation, "Jesus does not intend for us to be unafraid in the sense of 'buck up' and 'be strong'; on the contrary, he says that we should 'rest in him, take a load off, and be refilled for the journey.' "

Although the interaction of the women at the tomb with Christ oftentimes pales against more dramatic post-Resurrection encounters, it speaks directly to Jesus' ongoing message of the good news: *Don't be afraid.* But the conclusion of Jesus' message broadens the meaning by downplaying our fear and lifting up God's desire that we get on with the business of living. Jesus ends by saying, "Go tell my brothers to leave for Galilee, and they will see me there."

The scripture states that the women simply "went on their way." It is an odd, anticlimactic end to the encounter. Notice, though, that there is no mention of fear or of being overwhelmed. No, the presence of Christ addresses those emotions, and it is now time, once again, to begin the journey.

It occurs to me that the women in this passage and Frank have something very special in common. They all turned away from their fear, not because they necessarily conquered or rose above it, but because they chose to trust that God will keep the promise to direct our paths—indeed, to be waiting across the expanse of time and personally to meet us on the other side.

THE THIRD WORD

What are you so concerned about?

Luke 24:13-34

How Could You Not Know?

It was the talk of the day. Something dramatic had happened at the tomb, but what? A story about men in dazzling robes and a resurrection circulated through the community, but it all seemed very difficult to comprehend. Were people just caught in a hoax or possibly overwhelmed by the events of the past few days? Regardless, to think that Jesus had actually risen from the dead sounded, well . . . like nonsense.

Thus, for two of Jesus' followers to be in deep discussion about the day's activities was not surprising. They were so engrossed in their conversation, they nearly missed the stranger who had joined them on their journey to Emmaus. "What are you so concerned about?" the stranger asked. In sad and disbelieving tones, they told him, "You must be the only person in Jerusalem who hasn't heard about all the things that have happened in the last few days!" "What things?" replied the stranger. "The things that happened to Jesus, the man from Nazareth."

The men spent a few moments enlightening the stranger about who Jesus was and why he was important—somewhat of a "CliffsNotes" education for this clearly uninformed person. They talked about Jesus' prophecies, miracles, and apparent good favor with God and the people. Then, in short form, they told the stranger about the past few days. It was an unbelievable story that implicated the religious leaders and priests in what ultimately ended in Jesus' murder.

All the while, the stranger listened. After a short pause, the men continued, "We had thought he was the Messiah who had come to rescue

Israel...." Their incredible sadness had caused them to question every-thing, even the women's report of an empty grave. They wondered, *Could it be true? Do we dare believe in such things? But if we could only see him, talk to him, walk near him, then we could know for ourselves that what has happened is real.* No, their expectations of the Messiah had not turned out as they had hoped, but little did they know that God had something much better in store.

Jake

There is a difference between knowing the truth and comprehending it in your soul. After discovering his HIV status, Jake realized that telling the truth about his condition was not the issue; it was what people would do with the truth once they knew. A hemophiliac and struggling artist, Jake found himself placed between worlds embattled by the disease—the unsuspecting hemophiliac community and the fledgling artists of New Orleans, whose numbers of those testing positive increased by the day. As Jake would later confide, people considered him to be the only gay hemophiliac drug user around, thus almost ensuring that he would, in some way, at some point, test positive. The problem was that Jake was neither gay nor a drug user, although that did not prevent people from speculating. Once he discovered his HIV status, he concluded that trying to argue or explain was useless.

The late 1980s was a very difficult time for anyone with HIV. People's misunderstanding about the disease and the plethora of stereotypes surrounding the illness created a culture of fear that permeated every aspect of society. For hemophiliacs such as Jake and me, it was even more complicated. As *innocent victims* (an absurd and troubling term), we did not fit comfortably in predefined categories. The strongest HIV/AIDS coalitions formed from the gay and lesbian communities, whose battle for equal rights meshed with their concerns about the disease.

On the other side, Middle America was so afraid of the disease and stigma surrounding it, they saw hemophiliacs as unfortunate lepers caught in a tragic situation. And although two thousand years had passed since the time of Jesus, still no one dared touch a leper.

It is into this quagmire that Jake waded. Although Jake prided himself on trusting in the *goodness* of people, he soon discovered that we are fragile, failed human beings on whom fear and misunderstanding can have a powerful hold. Not long after discovering his condition, Jake lost his girlfriend and most of his straight acquaintances. Within a year, Jake's only companions were his fellow artists from Bourbon and Magazine streets and those he met at a local HIV support group.

Most disturbing for Jake was the reaction of the church he had attended for nearly two years. A devout Southern Baptist from an early age, Jake realized that cultivating a faithful religious life in New Orleans was difficult. However, an almost accidental invitation by a cab driver led Jake to a local Baptist church. At first only a sporadic attendee, Jake became a regular in the early morning worship service and started volunteering as an usher.

Two weeks after completing his first rotation on the usher schedule, Jake found himself at the emergency room of a local hospital complaining of shortness of breath and a high fever. The diagnosis was pneumocystis pneumonia, an opportunistic infection common in persons with AIDS. Three weeks, one hospital stay, and an HIV test later, Jake's life changed forever.

As fate would have it, Jake stood at the door of the church office, having arrived to confide in his pastor, and overheard the church secretary sharing an off-color joke about, as Jake would later recall, some asinine scenario involving an HIV-positive gay man, an Ethiopian, and a lion. (Jake never shared the punch line.) Transfixed in the doorway, Jake watched as his last opportunity for community seemed to fade away. He left without seeing the pastor and never returned to the church again. Jake later recalled how it wasn't the story so much as the approving laughter of the church staff and others that struck so deeply into his heart.

The power of *the secret* for a person living with HIV/AIDS can be overwhelming. I hear countless friends who live with the disease discuss the same feelings of uncertainty and fear when it comes to revealing their conditions. However, even greater than the secret is the burden of bearing it alone. Rejection is one thing; more painful is the apparent spiritual apathy that grips those unwilling to disrupt their lives to confront the magnitude of the disease and its effects. Thus, it becomes easier for many to make jokes, rationalize their prejudices, or even ignore the crisis than to confront the ramifications of the disease, for both themselves and the community of faith.

It would be nearly ten years before Jake would find his way back to a church. While teaching art at a local community college, Jake met a young, fresh-out-of-seminary associate pastor who shared not only his strange fascination with John Kennedy but also hemophilia and a HIV-positive diagnosis . Jake's newfound friendship revived his interest in faith and the church. Fighting off a decade of hard feelings and cynicism toward organized religion, Jake reignited, at least for a moment, his belief in the basic goodness of humanity. He started attending the church, became active in the choir, started dating a fellow art enthusiast, and volunteered at a local homeless shelter. Jake even taught Sunday school and helped develop a resource ministry for persons living with AIDS. But his journey home was filled with much uncertainty and, at times, incredible anger—not necessarily at God, but at those he met along the way, who so often were unaware of the holy strangers at their sides.

During my two-year friendship with Jake, I realized that his journey sounded all too familiar. Jake loved to quote from the 1994 movie *Swimming with Sharks,* in which Kevin Spacey's character states, "Life is not a movie. Everyone lies, good guys lose, and love does not conquer all." Jake watched it unfold time and again—people who talk about what Jesus would do but who clearly have no intention of living that way. As Jake liked to say, for those of us on the receiving end of such faithless bigotry, it is simply easier to walk away than walk through. In classic, historical fashion, the church missed a powerful opportunity to see Jesus in our midst during these early years of the AIDS crisis, by allowing so many people like Jake to simply walk away.

Jake helped me understand that, unfortunately and far too often, while trying to make sense of God's will or work in the world, we, the church, unknowingly cross paths with Jesus but are unable to celebrate that moment of *God with us.* Thus, in the third encounter following the Resurrection, it is no surprise that Jesus, on a fateful road to Emmaus, looked into the eyes of his two followers and called them fools. Literally and figuratively, they have been down that road before.

The Promises of God (John 16 and Beyond)

"In this world you will have trouble" (John 16:33 NIV). Jesus uttered these words to his disciples in the Gospel of John. The conversation was stark with talk of death, struggle, and persecution. He made the statement, not as some theoretical observation, but as a description of the reality that is unfolding all around them.

You will be tested, tortured, and scattered. Yes, you are scared. Yes, you are confused. Yes, you are even considering bolting. Yes, *in this world, you will have trouble.* The words must have been anticlimactic for some, completely unnerving for others. The disciples tried to appear strong. But their hearts responded differently. Jesus was giving them a glimpse over the precipice of time, and the questions began to rage: *What can he possibly mean? Is he toying with us? Of course, there will be trouble. Take a look around; it is everywhere!*

They were several miles into the journey now. It had been nearly three years since Jesus had first called them to follow him. They had seen miracles, healings, and even resurrections. Their identities as disciples were now sealed, and they must have wondered where the journey would lead.

Thus, the obvious shift in Jesus' tone created a sense of bewilderment and unease. For some, following Jesus involved more than dusty roads and front row seats to unbelievable events. However, none of them imagines the events that were to unfold.

Maybe this was the first time most of the disciples realized that following Jesus required real sacrifice. To travel with him, listen to his teachings, and watch his amazing gifts at work was one thing; but to experience life-changing, possibly *life-ending* sacrifice certainly was another.

Even Jesus' next words, preached for generations as a source of comfort in difficult times, must have been shocking: "But take heart, for I have overcome the world." *What? He just talked about persecution, sacrifice, and sorrows, and now he wants me to take heart?*

At this point, no one would accuse the disciples of being bold. But Jesus was asking them to take a gamble on his credibility. Earlier in the passage, the disciples responded by saying that they understood and really did believe. "Do you believe?" Jesus replied. "The time is coming when you will be scattered." This response surely stunned them. Jesus clearly insisted that they did not now understand; that what they would be called to risk was significant; and that their struggles were just beginning. "In this world you will have trouble . . . but (although you presently don't get it) take heart for I have overcome the world."

When Jesus called us to take a gamble on his credibility and to risk ourselves in his name, he did not take such a request lightly. In fact, scripture details one instance after another of God calling people to face a difficult world. The disciples would later understand the magnitude of Jesus' words and the stark price of following him. But they would also grasp the power of the risk and would eventually (with the exception of John) lay down their lives for Jesus. In spite of the tremendous cost, they learned to trust beyond the horizon of what they could see, to understand, and to take hold of God's promises. They realized that the same God who often required that we place our hearts and lives on the auction block also provided an assurance that bolstered our spiritual confidence and calmed our fears.

Scripture highlights several promises regarding our encounters with Jesus. Unlike many who take them for granted or rarely consider them at all, Jake clung to them as places of safety in an uncertain world. They were not simply words on a page or engagements for reflection; these promises served as his life preservers—a constant friend when all others vanished. They did not take away the fear of what the disease might do or even relieve the pain of everyday life, but they instilled a sense of hope that nothing, including AIDS, could steal.

Seeing the Messiah

Amazingly, Jake never lost his belief that Jesus is the Messiah, but he did lose hope in too many of the Messiah's followers. They could not fathom that the stranger in their midst knew very well about the struggles of life but also possessed an insight into faith that would have served them well, had they listened. Instead, most passed him by, unaware of the remarkable wisdom they were allowing to slip away.

Only two years into our friendship, Jake's journey on this earth ended. Standing at the graveside, I was amazed at the number of lives he had touched. Countless friends, acquaintances, and colleagues filled the small family cemetery to say good-bye to, as one attendee put it, the best friend anyone could ever have. Another mourner stated, "Every time we talked with him or enjoyed a meal together, there was an amazing sense of peace." I agree.

Jesus asked the two travelers, "What are you so concerned about? Can you not see who I am?" Fortunately, they realized in the breaking of bread that Jesus was, indeed, with them. This began a flood of emotions and feelings that stirred a new conversation about possibilities, and, later, these suppositions were confirmed by others who experienced similar things.

However, too often, the answer for those who encounter Jesus is still *no!* But, graciously, the journey continues, and God, as close as the next step, is waiting, that our eyes might be opened and our hearts strangely warmed. And, who knows, maybe the stranger in our midst might just understand our concerns and fears better than we and, all the more profound, be willing to share the burden of the load with us.

Unanswered Answered Prayers

A friend of mine told the story of her first Good Friday service. She had grown up in a denomination whose liturgical experiences were very limited. Thus, when she became a United Methodist, she immediately fell in love with the various rituals of the Christian year, especially the celebration of Holy Communion. She loved everything about it, including the moment of quiet reflection when she would meditate on the cross. The cross gave her a focal point and a deep sense of connection to Christ.

During this particular Good Friday service, the pastor served Communion to the congregation as part of a joint expression of Maundy Thursday and Stations of the Cross. When my friend arrived at the altar to receive Communion and view the cross, she realized that it had been covered in black drape in remembrance of Good Friday. She recounted how the sight of the cross hidden behind the cloth not only caught her off guard but also sent a deep sense of uneasiness throughout her soul. Where would she focus? How could she take Communion? How could she remember Jesus with the cross covered in such a way?

The story strikes me for its similarity to what the travelers must have felt on the road to Emmaus. *He was supposed to be the Messiah. To restore Israel. Where do we look now? Our prayers should not have gone unanswered!* At first reading, I know the travelers seemed self-centered or incredibly foolish—in fact, Jesus called them such. However, Jesus' words were not meant to degrade or deride them, but to push them beyond their despair and to help them see through the veil of their pain and disappointment. Most hopeful for me, though, is that God continues today to do that for each of us.

Has there ever been a time in your life when you believed God did not answer a prayer? Has there ever been a time when God answered a prayer in a way different from what you wanted or expected? The answer to both is probably yes; at least it is for me. Nothing can be more frustrating than to confront what one had thought were God's intentions, only to discover God working in a different way. However, in my life, each unanswered prayer turns out to be the answer itself. And God's intentions for my life, though different from what I had expected, are certainly richer than I could imagine.

Although the travelers to Emmaus felt disappointed that Jesus was not the sort of Messiah they had expected, they found a new perspective during that meal. Maybe for the first time in their lives, they understood the real meaning of the prophecies and the nature of who the Messiah would be. The despair and confusion on their journey seemed all too familiar. But it was also reassuring because it reminds each of us that, in spite of our misgivings and concerns, God is always present and truly cares.

What are you concerned about today? Has your world not turned out exactly as you had planned? Do you feel abandoned, frustrated, confused? Dear friend, don't lose heart! We may not know exactly where the journey will lead, but we can be sure of who travels with us.

THE FOURTH WORD

Peace be with you

Luke 24:35-43
John 20:19-29

Sirens and Flowers

In January 1999, Cary drove his car onto a railroad crossing and placed the gear in park. He had seen the caution lights start to blink moments earlier but, almost welcoming the danger, made his way into the path of the locomotive. For the next few moments he sat patiently, waiting to die.

Many wonder what would cause a young man in his midtwenties to do something so reckless. What most do not know is that Cary's life had become unbearable. With one disappointment after another, the strain and stress grew unmanageable. Friends described Cary as a normal young man who seemed a bit down and sometimes despondent about his circumstances. Hesitant to reach out to friends or family for help, he struggled to find peace within the heavy web of depression. Some saw glimpses of his decline, but no one could have imagined this.

As the train approached, the brakes began to squeal. The engineer blew the horn frantically. *What could possibly be wrong with this fellow?* he thought. Exasperated, he yelled, "Why won't he move?" It appeared that nothing could have stopped the unfolding tragedy.

Suddenly, almost miraculously, the car lurched forward. Pressing the accelerator, the driver peeled out from between the crossing guards. Moments later the train passed without damage—except perhaps to the engineer's emotional condition.

The police arrested the driver and charged him with reckless endangerment. When asked why he drove his car onto the crossing, he said he intended to commit suicide. However, moments before the train was to plow into his car, he claimed the voice of God said, "Your life is not over; don't finish it this way!" The man was convicted and later admitted to a local treatment facility for depression.

Contrast this incident with a story about little Emily and an amazing spring day filled with all the joy and expectations that new seasons bring. Emily's father, Ronnie, who enjoyed spending his free time working in the yard and doing odd jobs around the house, was a successful physician in a moderate-sized southern town. The father of three, Ronnie particularly enjoyed outside activities while in the company of his children. Their family was more than tight knit; they did life together. Often neighbors saw the entire family, side by side, engaged in some lazy-day activity.

One thing that most impressed onlookers was the deep spiritual nature exhibited by the children. From an early age, each child radiated a genuine love of God and spiritual connection. The entire family showed a sincere commitment to God and to one another—a true rarity in today's complicated world.

And so, on this particular spring day, three-year-old Emily turned a seemingly inconsequential moment into a holy experience. While tending to a patch of weeds growing in one of the flower gardens, Ronnie noticed Emily surveying a gardenia bush that had produced one simple bloom. After several minutes Emily turned to her father and said, "Daddy, I want to give that flower to God." Ronnie replied, "Well, sweetheart, instead of picking it, why not just say that God can have it? That will be a great gift."

Emily nodded in approval and then, in a very serious but sincere manner, turned around, faced the sky, and closed her eyes. A hushed silence ensued. It went on and on. Finally Ronnie was startled to hear Emily say, "You're welcome."

Ronnie knew that a holy moment had been born from the sincere and quite astute heart of a three-year-old, whose ability to listen to the voice of God had not been overwhelmed by the noise of this world. Oh, how God must have enjoyed that conversation!

Maybe there are three types of people in this world—those who hear God in the squealing brakes; those who hear God in the flowers; and those who refuse to hear God at all. But the real hope for humanity is that God continues to beckon. Whether in the bright light of day or the darkness of depression, God does not forget to call our names and bring us home.

Peace Be with You

As the disciples stood listening to the story of the two men who claimed to have encountered Jesus on the road to Emmaus, their hearts were about to explode. The hope of Jesus' being alive contradicted every worldly emotion they could imagine. And then, suddenly, there was Jesus, standing before them and offering a simple greeting: "Peace be with you"—not quite the Aramaic equivalent of "howdy," but a personal, common salutation. Nevertheless, the disciples recoiled with disbelief and fear.

"Why are you so frightened? Why do you doubt?" Jesus asked.

By this point, unlike for Mary or the men on the road, the "shock value" of Jesus' appearance had decreased. The disciples had heard about the wonderful events at Jesus' tomb. One testimony after another, along with a personal visit to the tomb itself by Peter and John, bore witness to the incredible, unfolding scenario—Jesus was alive!

Jesus reached out his hands and showed them the scars. "Look at the wounds!" he said. "Touch them! Make sure that I am not a ghost." Jesus implored them to realize that he was indeed present with them again. But, as is common when logic and faith collide, some of the disciples had never felt so disconnected from him in their lives.

Doubt does that. It severs the most intimate connections of our existence. As a result, it is one of the Adversary's greatest tools. Like a knife through hot butter, doubt cuts deep into our confidence and causes one spiritual malady after another—low self-esteem, lack of direction, anger, paranoia. Doubt knows what to do with our failures, watering those seeds of guilt until they are full-blown weeds. The disciples felt the pain of guilt, for none of them except John had remained at the cross. They all left, abandoning Jesus when the hour came. Even if Jesus were really alive, could they face him? Perhaps what was bothering them wasn't so much the uncertainty of whether Jesus was truly alive, but the deeper fear: what if he couldn't forgive them?

Kathryn

Was she an angel? This was my first thought the day I met Kathryn. Her eyes exhibited an unbelievable blue, but they were no match for her smile. She spoke with crisp words, punctuated by a dry, subtle laugh that made you laugh with her. Although only sixteen, she appeared much older, not because of her physical appearance, but for the intricate way she spoke of life and its many issues. Clearly intelligent, Kathryn could talk on any number of topics, from politics and religion (my favorites) to Southeastern Conference football. Being sixteen myself at the time, I was both intrigued and intimidated by this self-confident young woman. She was the kind of girl you either married or elected president.

We met in October 1986, at the University of Mississippi Medical Center in Jackson. I was undergoing a corneal transplant to correct an eye disease called keratoconus. Although I was born with the disease, my vision had deteriorated significantly the previous summer. A condition called hydrops (a ruptured membrane between the cornea and the pupil) required the transplant.

It was my first encounter with the children's hospital at the University of Mississippi Medical Center. In 1986, the facility was a circular multi-story building in which each floor had the same basic design. The nurses' stations were located in the middle, surrounded by pie-shaped hospital rooms just big enough to house a bed and a rocker. Remember, this was a children's hospital. It was also a state-run hospital, which meant the decor left a lot to be desired. However, since it was also a teaching hospital, the medical staff were among the best in the state.

I lived eighty miles south in the town of Hattiesburg but had come to Jackson when the local ophthalmologists decided that my hemophilia might complicate any transplant efforts. I was referred to one of the foremost corneal specialists in the Southeast, a small woman who looks more like your favorite aunt than a physician. (Her residents later told me that her image gave way to Patton or Attila the Hun when needed.)

The surgery went well. Almost immediately, my sight improved (relative, of course, to having no sight at all). However, I had to wear an eye patch and, with my sight very poor in the other eye, spent most of my time listening to cassette tapes or sitting quietly in my room. My emotional state was fragile at best. Although optimistic about the surgery, I did not like hospitals or being unable to take care of myself. The mixture of both proved difficult for everyone around me.

My hematologist was Indian and even smaller and feistier than my eye surgeon. She spoke with a heavy accent and was very direct. However, also like my ophthalmologist, she was extremely kind and very dedicated to her patients. Concerned that I was spending too much time moping in my hospital room, she suggested (or shall we say insisted) that I take a stroll around the ward. At first I protested profusely, but I was sternly booted out of bed by this four foot eleven drill sergeant in a doctor's coat.

It was on one of these strolls that I met Kathryn. I was taking one of my "protest runs" around the nurses' station (I had refused to go anywhere else in the hospital as a sign of civil disobedience) when I noticed a girl my age sitting on the edge of her bed. Her door was open, and she invited me in. As I stated earlier, the first things I noticed about Kathryn were her eyes and her smile. The next was the bandage around her head. As I would later discover, Kathryn suffered from an inoperable brain tumor. While other sixteen-year-old girls were worrying about what clothes they wore, who they dated, or the latest gossip around school, Kathryn spent most of her days dealing with treatments and resting. However, she attentively kept up with current events and, as her family would tell me, enjoyed dreaming about her career and "Mr. Right." Her positive attitude belied her condition. From the moment I met her, I was amazed by her ability to look beyond the despair of her illness and maintain hope.

Kathryn had been in the hospital many times during her illness. Although the doctors assured her family there was nothing they could to save her life, she continued fighting against the odds. She was a nurses' favorite, partly because of her attitude but also because, along with yours truly, she was the oldest "child" on the floor. Actually, all the nurses conceded that Kathryn had been in the hospital so much that she had become like a member of their families.

In addition to hope, faith was one of Kathryn's most noticeable attributes. She spoke of God in such personal terms that even the most ardent agnostic must have felt a connection. To Kathryn, her faith was not a crutch, but a part of life as necessary as breath. My self-pity quickly gave way to awe as this fellow sojourner encouraged, consoled, and prayed for me. Her unshakable optimism never failed to stun me. As I look back on our few, brief visits together, I cannot recall a time when Kathryn did not make me laugh or smile. I remember then, as now, wanting to achieve that kind of hope and faith in my own life.

One day close to the end of my stay, the cries from Kathryn's room became more alarming as her seizures worsened. Her pain must have been unbelievable. But the next day Kathryn, although weakened, showed the same grace and peace as before. Even after years of reflecting on those experiences, I still do not have the words to describe the courage and valor she displayed.

Our last conversation took place shortly after a church youth group visited our hospital ward. Expecting to find only small children, the group members, many of them our own age, dressed in costume for the purpose of handing out candy and other treats. Kathryn and I caused quite a stir as the visiting youth barged through our doors, only to find two of their peers sitting, somewhat overgrown, in our beds. The looks on their faces were priceless. But I remember every one of them regaining their composure long enough to try to cheer us up. Kathryn commented about the hilarious looks on their faces but also the obvious kindness in their hearts.

I am sorry to say I do not know what happened to Kathryn. When I returned to the hospital two months later for another eye surgery, no one could tell me about her. I asked everyone, but for one reason or another no one knew. It is as though she had vanished. But, her story changed the way I viewed life. How could someone with such trials and difficulties as hers possess such a beautiful perspective on the world? What was it deep inside Kathryn that caused her to look past the prickly and painful nature of the thorns she carried to celebrate their presence and live a life of genuine peace? I couldn't answer the questions. (I still find them difficult.) And, yet, even as a sixteen-year-old boy, I knew I would not be the same again.

Too Much "Us"

The nature of God's peace has nothing to do with relinquishing the world's difficulties; it has everything to do with embracing the world's beauty. Why does a three-year-old recognize the voice of God in a flow. garden, while a twenty-five-year-old must look over the edge of life itself before hearing *it?* One answer can be found by comparing what the world tells us is real and what God has placed in our souls.

In the encounter with Jesus described above, I do not believe that every disciple moves back from Jesus when he appears in the room. While most retreat, maybe just one recognizes Jesus and draws closer. Yes, he looks at the wounds, maybe even touches them, but more importantly he hears that voice, and he knows who is speaking. My contention is that he would not respond that way out of choice, as one who might have control over the decision, but rather out of a place deep within where God is working and speaking, a place resurrected, if you will, from our spiritual childhood. God has no trouble carrying on conversations with three-year-olds, *because three-year-olds have not yet been convinced that they can be their own gods.* Let me say it another way: The nature of God's peace is never experienced in our self-sufficiency, but only in a relationship resembling the dependence of a child on a parent. Our "mortality" is not the result of wounds to our bodies, but in the scars, scabs, and scratches of our souls that become infected with too much "us" and not enough "God."

Thomas

If Luke's version of the fourth word does not prick our souls, John's certainly will. Having been absent at the first meeting with Jesus, Thomas refused to believe that Jesus was risen until he saw and touched the wounds. Over the years, the term "doubting Thomas" has been a target of criticism. In truth, though, Thomas was neither a coward nor a doubter; more accurately, he was weary. Having prepared himself for the kingdom of God, only to watch the unraveling of his hopes and dreams, Thomas must have come to feel the burden of responsibility for sunrise, sunset, and everything else in between.

Thomas did not stand as an impediment to faith or to Jesus; more than anything, and much like the rest of us, he was simply an impediment to himself. Have you ever wanted to believe but, because of one heartache or another, simply could not bring yourself to do it?

"Touch me. Place your finger in my wounds," Jesus exhorted Thomas. As Thomas drew back his hand from Jesus' body, his words said it all: "My Lord and my God!" The look on Thomas's face conveyed even more. I imagine his expression, a mixture of incredible excitement and paralyzing shame, part joy, part apology, and part regret. At this moment, no character of the Bible is more human.

For Those Who Have Not Seen

A pastor friend of mine told the story of a trip to a personal-care spa (or "boot camp," as she called it) in the middle of the Utah desert. Having neither desired nor needed the trip for herself, she made it as a gesture of kindness and support of a good friend. However, she still participated in the daily routines, which included a six-mile hike in the desert heat. After several days of activities, my friend found herself in need of, as she put it, an emergency pedicure.

While talking with the pedicurist, my friend was amused by the young lady's story of a successful pastor who visited her department several months earlier.

"I remember him because he was so depressed," the lady said. "I couldn't get him to acknowledge me or anything that I suggested. Finally, after trying several times to make small talk, I jokingly asked if he would like for me to paint his toenails red." The woman laughed and continued, "To my amazement, he agreed, and I did it—I painted his toenails red!"

By this time my friend, who admitted to a brief moment of daydreaming herself, was listening intently.

The woman continued, "He paid the fees, got up, and walked out. I was convinced that I would never hear from him again. Then, just this morning, he called back. You will never believe what he told me!"

It seemed that the pastor had reason to be depressed. He told the pedicurist that after seeing his church grow to a significant size, he had largely abandoned his own soul. The objectives of his earthly ministry had overshadowed his obligations to his health, his family, and his emotional well-being. His fire, momentum, and inner peace slowly ebbed away, and, at the urging of family and friends, he took a break to try to make sense of it all. Somehow he found his way to the Utah desert and wandered into the pedicurist's shop.

He confessed that, following his visit, he almost went back and asked to have the polish removed, but he was afraid of causing a scene and embarrassing himself and her. Not knowing how to remove it himself, he went home, polished digits and all. On Sunday morning the pastor arrived back at his church. When he made his way into the large sanctuary, he began to think about the absurdity of the past few days. Even more absurd was the fact that he, the pastor of one of the most powerful churches in the country, was standing in front of his congregation with red toenails underneath his black wingtips and silk socks. He told the pedicurist that he began to smile. The smile turned into a grin, and by the time he started to preach, his soul had become downright giddy.

The pastor emerged from his depression a changed man. Not only did he change careers, leaving the pastorate for the mission field, but also he reconnected with family and friends. His life made sense again, and all because of the Utah desert and red toenail polish. As with Thomas, God uses the tangible and sometimes ridiculous things of this world—things we touch, smell, and see—to ignite belief.

Thomas Revisited

Jesus, finally recognized by Thomas, told him, "Blessed are you, but even more blessed are those who believe and have not seen." At first this sounded like a rebuke, but Jesus was only stating the fact of real peace. As mentioned earlier, the real goal of God's relationship with us is that we might believe and not require a constant reminder that God's presence, in, around, and about us is sufficient for our deepest and most pervasive moments of need. Even our failures cannot prevent us from receiving God's love. God simply won't stand for it! We mean too much to the Creator. Paul is right: "I'm absolutely convinced that nothing— nothing living or dead, angelic or demonic, today or tomorrow, high or low, thinkable or unthinkable—absolutely *nothing* can get between us and God's love because of the way that Jesus our Master has embraced us" (Romans 8:38-39 Message).

Dear friends, this is our spiritual birthright. It is why three-year-olds carry on casual conversations with the sky. It is why terminally ill girls remember to smile. It is why the pomposity of religion pales in comparison with simple glimpses of God. And it is why all of us, created in God's own image, pause at the sound of *that voice*, even when we cannot figure out why. When the doubts, failures, and fears of this world come crashing in around us, we have the assurance of Jesus' own scars and wounds. Touch them!

Go into the world

Matthew 28:18-20
Mark 16:15-18
Luke 24:45-49

The Great Commission

This is not like the other times. Before, when Jesus sent his disciples, there was always a temporary feeling attached. They would go, usually two by two, and visit the neighboring towns or villages, preach the message of redemption, and then eventually make their way back to sit at the feet of the Master. Complete with instructions for how to handle almost every situation they might encounter, the disciples felt competent and able, and also assured of returning to the counsel of Jesus.

However, as they stood on the mountain for this particular gathering, the exchange felt more permanent and exceptionally broad in scope. The disciples had a new mission, as well as a new set of criteria to employ and by which to measure their effectiveness. *Make disciples, teach, baptize* are Matthew's recollections. Mark, probably from Peter's memory, adds a discourse about snakes and the ability to heal those who are ill. Luke's history records the coming power of the Holy Spirit and how that allows the disciples to be witnesses to the work and intention of Christ's ministry. Regardless of the specifics, each passage possesses a common theme—*go!* The disciples' ministry was no longer bound by the regions of Galilee and Judea. The scope was changing, and the disciples were held personally responsible for it.

Where would this commission send them? What would they

encounter along the journey? How would they survive so far from familiar surroundings? Could they do this without the watchful and waiting presence of Jesus? What about the message? Were they able; were they really willing? The questions mounted.

For many, the Great Commission texts are a call to arms, more militaristic than personal for the church. But to read the Commission texts, one must paint the entire picture. The scene unfolds, not against the backdrop of an eager army, but rather in a group of fragile human beings who struggle to live out extraordinary teachings amidst very ordinary lives and fears. In every Commission text, the prior passage details a strong sense of doubt or insecurity among the disciples. The disciples portrayed in these texts are less concerned about the world they would transform, and more intent on how their own worlds might change.

Urban Cowboy with a Cross

The church of my youth typifies many small-town congregations. Founded nearly a hundred years ago, it has been operated and cared for by successive generations of the same families. Occasionally newcomers will make their way into positions of leadership, but with every change of pastor the "new blood" fades away and the long-established power structures resurface. The church is traditional in ways common to most small-town congregations—theologically conservative and male-led.

However, also typically, the church consists of many good people. Hard-working and caring, they faithfully live out life together. Growing up, I remember our closest friends were always church members. We often ate Sunday lunch together and shared fellowship regularly. It was a close-knit family of believers.

It is in this church that my faith was born and formed. My family attended church regularly, never missing a worship service or special event. By age nine, I was convinced that every proper church had Sunday school, Sunday morning and evening worship, and a prayer meeting on Wednesday nights.

It was about this time that Tom came to be our pastor. A fiery orator, Tom had a passion for preaching the gospel in animated tones and gestures. Although somewhat scary to a nine-year-old, Tom's oratory was spellbinding if not downright exhausting—he could preach for an hour without breaking a sweat. His sermons captivated my church during his five years as pastor, and it was during his tenure that I was baptized.

Contrasting with his larger-than-life presence in the pulpit, Tom was quiet and reflective in person. This added to a unique aura that kept people wondering what he was thinking. Initially convinced that his quiet demeanor was the result of spiritual concentration, I later discovered that Tom was simply shy. His oratory provided a release for what was otherwise a reserved nature. Very pleasant and humorous once you got to know him, Tom's personality conveyed a sense of real-world living. The combination of a powerful pulpit style and a real-world attitude connected Tom to those inside and outside the church.

I vividly remember one of Tom's converts, a young man named Jimmy. Jimmy came to our town to work in the local chicken hatchery as a gender specialist. His job was literally to predict the gender of the baby chicks prior to their hatching, which in the poultry business is important. Thus, though many did not know it, getting a job as a gender specialist was a lucrative career move, especially for a young single such as Jimmy. With the world by the tail and some change in his pocket, Jimmy lived a good life and, as it turned out, a rather hair-raising one.

The time was 1980, and the disco era was in full force. The Bee Gees were heirs to the Beatles, and John Travolta was king of the entertainment world. One movie that inspired a generation (or at least seriously disrupted their fashion choices) was *Urban Cowboy*, a story about a young urban man's attempt to adopt the remnants of cowboy culture. The hero, played by King John himself, spent most of his time at the world's largest honky-tonk, Gilley's, in Pasadena, Texas, riding a mechanical bull and watching urbanites parade around as cowboys, complete with boots, hats, and large belt buckles. Jimmy loved the movie and saw himself as a kind of cross between John Wayne and Barry Gibb.

From the congregation's founding in the late 1880s, our church had been very traditional and ordered. So for Jimmy to begin attending worship there was quite a surprise. It turned out he had been invited by a young woman whom he had met during a beauty pageant at a local college. An attractive young man, Jimmy never had any trouble finding dates, and he constantly attracted ladies' attention. Therefore, Jimmy's visit had little to do with religion and a great deal to do with a five foot five brunette named Sheila.

His arrival was spectacular, to say the least. He drove a brand-new yellow Nissan 200ZX and pulled into a space on the front row of the parking lot. Jimmy stepped out of his vehicle wearing a light blue leisure suit with western fringe, alligator boots, and a belt buckle engraved with the words, *They can have my gun when they pry it from my cold, dead fingers.*

However, two unexpected things happened to Jimmy during his first visit. First, Sheila came down with a significant case of mononucleosis and was unable to attend the service. Second, he was shaken by Tom's message. The sermon began with a question: "And so, what do you believe you are put here on earth to accomplish?" Jimmy later recalled being amazed at how Tom *spoke directly to him.* After the service, Jimmy stopped Tom and asked, "Do you really believe that everyone has a God-given purpose?" Tom replied, "If we are made by God, we are made for a reason."

Jimmy returned the next Sunday. Over the ensuing weeks, Tom spent a great deal of time with Jimmy, sharing with him God's intentions for making the most of our time on this planet and encouraging him to, as Tom loved to say, "live significantly." Jimmy thought this was exactly what he had been doing, but the witness inside of him now said something different. Three months after his first Sunday visit, Jimmy was baptized and joined the church. A delight to be around, Jimmy quickly shed the urban cowboy image and found himself amazed to learn about a God who was reaching out to him and wanted him to participate in a greater plan. The deeper the discussion, the more Jimmy heard God calling.

One of the most memorable conversations of my life took place as Jimmy sat with my family around our dinner table. Tom was also present, along with several friends from the church. Food was everywhere, and for most of the evening the conversation was light and entertaining. Sometime around the last piece of fried chicken being eaten, Jimmy looked up and said, "I believe God is calling me to the mission field." The room grew silent. "In fact," he continued, "I know God is calling me to go home and preach the gospel."

The first person to react was my mother, who got up from her chair, walked over to Jimmy, put her arms around him, and said, "Oh, we are so proud of you." Others hugged Jimmy, high-fived, or shouted congratulations. Tom was especially proud. Not so happy about it myself, I blurted out, "But, why can't you preach here?" My best friend, who was sitting by me, elbowed me in the side and said incredulously, "Because God told him to go home, you idiot!" Jimmy laughed, then looked over at his fiancée—you guessed it—Sheila.

The last time we heard from Jimmy and Sheila, they were teaching and working in remote villages in Japan. However, the distance from Mississippi to Japan cannot compare with the distance Jimmy traveled to find real meaning in life. To this day, I still remember his words: *Sometimes our mission field is around the world and sometimes it is our home.*

A Town Called Seminary

Just off the hustle and bustle of Highway 49 in south Mississippi sits the town of Seminary. Its main street is a collection of diners, gas stations, and memories of days gone by. The local school is the town hub, fulfilling the function not only of educating the children but also of providing a majority of the town's social outlets. The people exhibit a strong sense of community, with deep Christian values. They are exceptionally kind to one another. The pace is slow, and people like it that way.

My connection to Seminary is unique. I did not grow up there, nor do I have family who live there. In fact, I have spent less than two hours within the city limits. However, this community played an important part in my life and helped shape my ministry for years to come.

I went there in 1994. I was completing a degree at Duke Divinity School and was preparing to take my first full-time appointment in The United Methodist Church. In April, I received word that I had been appointed to Seminary UMC. I was excited and, admittedly, somewhat nervous about the appointment.

In Seminary, the rumor hit on a Sunday morning. Talk had it that the new pastor was HIV-positive. Although this fact was not a secret, the district superintendent had thought it wise not to share the news with the congregation. Instead, they learned it by way of rumor, and the rumor made its way to the church's governing board. After a full day of debate and questions, the board voted not to accept me as their new pastor.

On Monday I drove from North Carolina to Hattiesburg to visit my parents, unaware of what had taken place. My covenant meeting in Seminary was scheduled for Tuesday evening. (This is the traditional first meeting between a church and its new pastor.) When I arrived at my parents' house in Hattiesburg, I received the news from my wife, who had been informed by the district superintendent earlier in the day. We were shocked, hurt, and disappointed. But it was also one of the most intimate moments in our marriage. My wife and I shared our concerns about the future and together decided to trust God.

The next day, the bishop asked me to attend the planned covenant meeting. He clearly did not expect me to be appointed as pastor, but, as he stated later, he felt that I needed to go for the integrity of the process. Although it was a difficult decision, I agreed to go.

The meeting was uncomfortable at best. Those who decided to attend expressed sadness and dismay at the situation. The majority of my opposition was not present.

As I sat there, what began as discomfort, confusion, and anger quickly turned into compassion as I came face to face with the family of God in crisis—not just crisis over the appointment of a pastor, but a crisis of the soul. Over the course of my ministry I remembered this meeting as a precursor to what I would find in many lives, not to mention in my own. The fragile nature of God's children does not alter our responsibility to seek God's guidance and then live faithfully in its light. The people of this congregation had, for one reason or another, lost sight of what it meant to "be sent." Instead, they sought a guarantee that we somehow could faithfully live out the Great Commission on one hand and control where it might lead us on the other. Oh, how they wanted it to be different, but they were unprepared to make it so.

In that moment, I realized that the meeting was more for them than for me. They were in turmoil, and God had sent me to remind them of grace. When I left the meeting, I was convinced that it had been one of the most profound experiences of my life. In the years since, not a day has gone by that I haven't considered the uniqueness of that encounter, not only for my past but also for how I presently minister in the world. Truly in that moment the scripture came to life: *What the world had intended for evil, God had transformed for good.*

As I mentioned earlier, I spent only two hours in Seminary, Mississippi. The first hour was in 1994; the second, several years later. While driving from Jackson, I suddenly found myself in the Seminary UMC parking lot between the sanctuary and parsonage—the same parsonage in which they had been frightened for me to live. I sat there for an hour, gazing at the church and watching the people go by. It was a peaceful if somewhat surreal time. I allowed my mind to wonder about what could have been if the people had let me serve there. As I pondered the question, I realized that God's plan had not been thwarted or changed but actually had been fulfilled.

For me, the real purpose of the event was not to mark a failure, but to celebrate the power of God's work in *going*, even when it means going where you are not wanted. Sitting there in the car, I became convinced that God did not intend or predestine the congregation to reject my ministry, but also that God did not miscalculate the power of the Spirit's presence in the midst of it. This truth reminded me that God is faithful and present even when we are unwilling to accept that fact.

I can only imagine what Jesus felt on Calvary when he looked down at his followers and realized that they didn't get it either. The sermons, the hope, the promise—all of it dwindled in the face of misguided intentions. Human tendency is to call it off. Not only were the people unreceptive of God's grace but also they were unworthy of it, as are we. And yet Jesus responded by saying, "Forgive them, for they do not understand."

"Go"

Though there was much the disciples did not comprehend, they understood Jesus' message of *go*. For the previous three years they had been on a seemingly endless journey, first leaving the familiarity of family, friends, and vocation, and then moving to a deeper place in Jesus' teaching and plan. They knew what it meant to go because Jesus had sent them out before in preparation for the real event. That event was taking place now.

This fifth word does not represent the final encounter of Jesus with his disciples; it does, however, indicate a shift in Jesus' emphasis and theme. The previous four encounters focused on the disciples' personal reactions and their emotions, fears, and uncertainties. But with the fifth encounter, Jesus had moved to a more outward focus that eventually became the theme of his final moments on earth.

Perhaps this encounter signaled to the disciples that Jesus would not remain with them for much longer. An urgent, instructive tone surfaces here and remains through the Ascension. Jesus was preparing the disciples for more than just the beginning of their ministry; he was preparing them for life without him. For me, this process seems akin to the parental rite of sending one's children into the world. The excitement and joy of new beginnings is naturally mixed with deeper emotional struggles that any change or uncertainty brings.

My first real experience of these mixed emotions occurred when my wife and I moved from Mississippi to North Carolina so I could attend Duke Divinity School. For our entire lives we had lived within thirty miles of our family and friends. Now, nearly eight hundred miles from home, we were scared to death. I will never forget when the last car of family members pulled away from our apartment. As we watched it disappear over the horizon, it dawned on us that we were on this journey alone. Yes, there was excitement about our new adventure, but at that moment the overwhelming feeling was one of loneliness. I know now that the only cure for the natural fears that arise from being sent is in the going itself—the medicine that the passage of time brings, and the confidence that your journey means something. It was a lesson that the disciples, like all of us, had to learn personally.

A Deeper Meaning

What eventually happened to each disciple is a matter of some debate and conjecture. However, aside from historical perspective and supposition, one fact is clear: From this small band of believers came the most significant religious movement in history. Not one of the disciples could imagine what their small movement looks like today. Granted, not all Christian influence has been productive or holy in nature. However, no one can dispute that the Christian movement has profoundly affected human existence. As the message developed, so did the institution, sometimes under attack, other times on the prowl. But the small band of eleven undoubtedly and unequivocally changed the course of the world.

Even more profound are the ways that the church changes the potential and possibility of the human experience. Imprinted on our souls is the image of a Creator whose love for us goes beyond life itself, reaching into the grave to restore our eternities. Every word or deed that marks and proclaims the good news provides a glimpse of Jesus.

Why were the disciples willing to go, even when they clearly did not understand what going might mean? Perhaps they realized that in going to share with others, they were in essence validating the imprint of God within themselves—closing the circle, if you will, on the wonderful cycle of grace, forgiveness, and salvation. They discovered that much of the path had been laid for them; that the directions were clearer than they suspected; and that the final destination was more wonderful and complete than they could imagine. Yes, there were roadblocks, obstacles, toils, and snares, but in the end it is an amazing journey.

And so that is why we go as well, knowing that we can experience the same cycle of grace, forgiveness, and salvation. Some go to faraway lands; others go across the street. Some go into hostile territories; others are called to go into their own homes and communities. Some find receptive hearts and minds; others find war, pain, and discontent. Some will discover fields ripe for harvest; others will toil for one small patch of fertile ground. We have all the same uncertainties, fears, and concerns as our brothers and sisters before us, but, like them, we go because we are sent.

For many, the thought of evangelism leaves us nervous and concerned. But truly witnessing to the good news of Jesus Christ has little to do with faraway lands or knocks on a stranger's door, and everything to do with our willingness to live our lives faithfully in the world. George Barna reports that 75 to 90 percent of all people who come to know Christ will do so through a friend or a relative. These reassuring statistics confirm the most successful evangelism program the world has ever known; in fact, it is the program Jesus himself employed. No offense to Billy Graham, but the greatest evangelists in the world are our mothers, sisters, brothers, uncles, best friends, and, yes, ultimately, potentially, you and me. *Go make disciples!*

THE SIXTH WORD

Have you caught any fish?

John 21:1-23

It amazes me how much of Jesus' ministry took place around the Sea of Galilee. So many encounters and engagements happened within a stone's throw of the place where he called those first followers. It was an incredible journey, but also one filled with many uncomfortable and troubling events.

Now, the Crucifixion and the events surrounding it had altered permanently the direction of the disciples' lives. And yet, given this unfolding drama, they still made their way to the sea, to launch their boats and cast their nets. Early one morning, after a long night's work, they looked up to see a vaguely familiar but unrecognizable figure standing on the shore.

"Did you catch any fish, my friends?" the man called out.

"No!" was Peter's reply.

The man said, "Then cast your nets on the other side, and you will catch plenty of fish!" The disciples did as he instructed, and the catch was so great that they had trouble lifting it into the boat.

Prompted by the familiarity of the scene, John suddenly focused and realized that the figure was Jesus. The last time Jesus performed such a miracle, Peter felt so unworthy that he knelt in shame. This time, however, Peter's joy at the sight of Jesus propelled him over the side of the boat and into the water, where he swam furiously to shore.

When the other disciples rowed to shore, they found a campfire already burning, complete with grilled fish and cooked bread.

"Bring me some of the fish you've caught," said Jesus. Peter did so, and Jesus replied, "Now sit, my friends, and let's have some breakfast together." To the disciples, it all seemed so familiar and it all seemed so right.

Jesus must have enjoyed the setting as well. By re-creating the scene from the first days of their ministry together, he knew the significance of the moment would not be lost on the disciples. Before, they were called to leave everything and follow him; now, they were being called to lay down not only their vocations and worldly pursuits but also eventually their lives. The meal they shared wasn't just breakfast; it was sacrament.

I can't help thinking that their time together was also lively and fun. Maybe they discussed humorous situations from their three-year journey, possibly recounting such stories as the time someone actually climbed a tree to get a glimpse of Jesus. Maybe James asked, "What was that fellow's name again?" Possibly Matthew answered, "You are talking about Zacchaeus, a former colleague of mine." Or maybe Thomas recalled the time Jesus berated the Pharisees over their lack of sincerity. Did he say, laughingly, "I still can't believe you called them hypocrites, and to their faces, no less!"?

From the edge of the circle, maybe Andrew added, "Yeah, but they couldn't have been as surprised as we were when the fish and loaves kept multiplying. People just kept eating. Remember how Judas..." Perhaps he stopped, and the group fell silent momentarily.

This was a gathering of comrades, reunited with their teacher and friend. Some scholars characterize this encounter as some sort of theological pep talk or relegate it to a simple lead-in for Jesus' conversation with Peter, but it was far more than that. Amidst the crackling fire, old stories, toasted bread, and roasting fish, a holy connection was born anew. Sometimes we forget that what happened between Jesus and his disciples, before canonized as our scriptures, was their story.

Learning to Lean

A few years ago, while I was taking my oldest daughter to school, she asked, "How did you and Mommy meet?" It was the first time that she had asked that question, and I realized it had been years since I spent any significant time thinking about it. Because our drive to school usually took twenty minutes, I had time to recount the moment when her mother and I first noticed each other. She giggled a great deal, rolled her eyes, and then graciously changed the subject. I guess she was not looking for such a long answer to a simple question.

However, the conversation sparked reflection on the blessings of my marriage and family. During the next few days, we pulled out pictures, told stories, and reminisced about long-forgotten memories and situations. My wife and I talked about everything from our first date to our first kiss to our first child. I told the girls stories about how beautiful their mom was the night I picked her up for our senior prom and how, three years later, I asked her to marry me. Of course, there was more giggling and eye-rolling, but there were also a lot of smiles and tears. Not only was it good for us; we knew this time of reflection was also important for our children. It gave them a glimpse into the story of their mom and dad's love for each other and, thus, of our love for them.

We looked back on that time of reflection as a refreshing opportunity to celebrate our life together. My wife and I had a wonderful time; our children simply felt we had gone over the edge. Every meal was a trip down memory lane, and our family movie night became *The Mom and Dad Video Hour.*

Thankfully, the family reruns stopped, which was probably a testament to the power of our daughters' prayers. However, what did not end was a new appreciation for remembering and sharing the formative moments of our family's life. We resolved to spend more time celebrating our journey, without, of course, making anyone miserable. The kids are very thankful.

A Conversation with Peter

As breakfast on the shore drew to an end, Jesus turned to Peter and quite unexpectedly asked, "Peter, do you love me?" Obviously, Peter was caught off-guard by the question. Of course, we do not know Peter's exact thoughts, but we assume a myriad of issues ran through his mind: *Why is Jesus asking this? Have I done something wrong? Does this have anything to do with the denial? Is he testing me?*

Peter answered, somewhat dazed, "Yes, Lord, you know that I love you." Jesus replied, "Then feed my lambs."

Several moments later, Jesus asked again, "Peter, do you love me?" Again Peter responded, "Yes, Lord, you know that I love you."

"Then take care of my sheep," Jesus again replied.

We can almost sense Peter's anxiety and frustration starting to rise. Then, for a third time, Jesus asked, "Peter, do you love me?"

One can hear the echo of Peter's dismay as he responded, "Lord, you know all things, you know I love you."

Jesus drew closer and said, "Then feed my sheep." And, in one final, dramatic moment, he whispered, "Follow me." Everyone sat in silence as they witnessed once again Jesus' call to move beyond the familiar and go forth in his name.

Over the next few verses of John's account, Jesus gave Peter a glimpse into his future and how things would change. Peter's life would no longer be his own. In following Jesus, Peter needed absolute and complete trust in him. One interesting nuance of the passage is that Peter's final response to Jesus included the Greek word *agapao* to describe the kind of love that Peter had for Jesus. The previous responses used a different Greek word, *phileo*, which is more a love between friends. *Agape* literally means a type of love that is unconditional and without boundaries. It is all-consuming and without restriction or expectation. To love this way is to abandon the notion of self-interest and to trust in God's all-consuming plan. Ultimately, it means to trust God with everything one has (W. E. Vine, Merrill F. Unger, and William White, Jr., *Vine's Expository Dictionary of Biblical Words* [Nashville: Thomas Nelson Publishers, 1985], 382).

The disciples were in new territory. They realized that their time around the campfire was meant to inspire in them passion for their common narrative. Their unique journey together gave their friendship depth and breadth, building among them a covenant of both experience and purpose. This narrative defined them and provided solace for the difficult road ahead. And yet the narrative also bid them to *go*. To love Jesus means to follow him. To follow him means to go into the world. To go into the world means to reach those who have, for so long, been unreachable. To reach the marginalized means transforming—no, revolutionizing—the way of the world. They do not own the gospel; they are merely the vessels for sharing it. Rich and poor, young and old, male and female, slave and free, Jew and Gentile—so many fish, and it is now time to cast to the other side.

A Common Story

Have you ever watched children at a birthday party? When allowed just to be themselves, children transform any room, playground, or gymnasium into a fantasy world of castles and exciting adventures. They talk, run, laugh, cry, and fuss, and through it all they live life fully, squeezing a full portion of existence from every tear and giggle. The reason most people reflect on their childhood with fondness and can share it openly with those whom they have never met is because we all experience those moments—being king, princess, or pirate.

In a similar way, God provides us with a common story. From the beginning of time until Christ's return, God's plan is interwoven through human existence, so that, for example, unsuspecting shepherds in the ninth century B.C. are intimately connected to fishermen after the turn of the millennium. What a picture this must be! And, best of all, we are a part of it—now!

I believe that every time the family of God gathers to worship, our common story should come to life. We sing, speak, and pray the words of our spiritual ancestors, and for that moment a simple room or gymnasium is transformed into a temple and complete strangers become best friends.

When I see my children playing, I wonder what it would be like to be transported to their world, where paychecks and appointments do not matter. Oh, how many times I have wanted to jump into Juli Anna's "Doodle Bug" electric car and hit the open road. But, knowing that Juli Anna would tell me that I am too big, I stand there and smile, realizing that I am connected to my children by more than just parenthood, but by my childhood as well.

How pleased God must be around that heavenly campfire, and in every moment that the church gathers, when God's children realize that they are connected—that they were never truly alone, forsaken, or abandoned, and in the end, it all meant something. I believe that God stands there as a proud parent, nudges Jesus, and smiles (Shane Stanford and

Ronnie Kent, *Salt and Light: Twenty-five Days for Making Life Matter*
[Longwood, FL: Xulon Press, 2003], 137-40).

The Full Table

Not long ago, I preached a series of revival sermons at a church
located in a small southern town. The town, incorporated 150 years earlier, is the site of one of the most important battles of the Civil War.
Throughout the downtown area are monuments dedicated to Con-
federate soldiers, indicating the deep and personal feelings many of the
townspeople still have. The community also has a history in the civil
rights movement, serving as a stopover in 1963 for Martin Luther King,
Jr., and his associates. As the locals recall, he stayed with a leading
African American family that lived just on the outskirts of town. Because
of fear for his safety, his presence was kept a secret.

As the years rolled on, times changed dramatically. However, most
churches remained resistant to significant racial progress. People talked
about equality and inclusiveness, but local congregations were some of
the only segregated institutions left in town.

The final night of the revival, I preached a sermon entitled "Come to
the Table." The focus of the message was the various occasions in scripture when God used a meal or table to provide meaningful life lessons.
My scripture text on this particular evening was the Last Supper. Using
the image of Jesus gathering his disciples around the table as a model for
modern Christian community, I asked the pastor to set a dinner table at
the front of the sanctuary, complete with silverware, fine china, and
stemware. Throughout the message, I invited various members of the
audience to come to the table. It is an illustrative tool I have used before,
and it serves me well.

The final part of the message highlights Jesus' call for us not only to
enjoy the table ourselves but also for each of us to go and invite others to
join. Thus, each person I invite is then asked to go into the congregation
and bring back a new tablemate. It is a moving scene, as men and women,
young and old make their way, hand in hand, to the table.

I took a few steps down the aisle and made a point of looking back at
the table. My comment was simple: "Doesn't the table of Christ look

THE SEVENTH WORD

Wait for the gift

Acts 1:1-11

Acts and a Friend Named Theophilus

Most modern descriptions of Jesus' final moments, including those in television, books, and movies, serve as forgettable postscripts to the birth, death, and resurrection. Even in the Gospel that bears his name, Luke affords the Ascension little more than a short paragraph, seemingly downplaying the event as a forgone conclusion to the true meaning of Jesus' earthly ministry. Mark's description is equally brief, while Matthew and John discuss it not at all. Realizing these facts, it is easy to understand why the details of the Ascension have been glossed over or completely forgotten in most modern renderings of the event.

However, as Luke begins the book of Acts, the story of the early church in a second letter to a friend named Theophilus, his account of the Ascension becomes both personal and significant, as though the author is struck with a renewed need for Christians to grasp the Ascension's place in the overall story of Jesus. This may have been because, with the book of Acts being written near the end of the age of the apostles, the second generation of Christians, Luke believed, needed a fresh knowledge of the Ascension.

However, maybe the answer is more pragmatic, not to mention more spiritual, in nature. Possibly Luke saw the book of Acts as the second part of the *real* narrative. To use Luke's own words, the gospel is a beginning, not a conclusion. Acts serves as a continuation of the good news, not necessarily through the physical work of Christ himself, but through Christ's body, the church.

The story needs a linchpin or bridge that can serve as the connection between the ministry of Jesus and the ministry of Christ's body. Maybe for Luke, the Ascension story becomes that linchpin. Perhaps his brief treatment of it in the Gospel wasn't intended to downplay the Ascension at all but to emphasize and focus on the profound doubt of the disciples. Did Luke fear that without first discussing their doubt, we might take for granted their embracing of the Holy Spirit? Whatever the answer, by Acts 1, Luke was ready to focus on the Ascension and, in the church's first book of history, to share with us one final encounter with Jesus.

The more interesting question for me, though, is *who is Theophilus?* Many scholars conclude that Theophilus is indeed a real person, possibly a Roman official and obviously a committed, Christian friend to Luke. However, realizing the subtleties of language employed throughout scripture, I can't help believing that, even if Theophilus was a real person, Luke tried to convey a deeper meaning.

First, Theophilus literally means *lover of God.* In other words, Luke addressed his works, which represent nearly thirty percent of the New Testament, to someone whose very name embodies its overall message. The Gospel of Luke and the book of Acts were clearly written to Christians and were never intended to serve simply as works of conversion, but also as works of instruction and encouragement.

Second, there was a shift in Luke's relationship with Theophilus between the writing of the Gospel to the writing of Acts. In the Gospel, Luke addressed Theophilus as "most honorable," indicating a more formal relationship. However, in the introduction to Acts the greeting was personal and intimate: "Dear Theophilus." Could it be, given the weaving of the Holy Spirit through the encounters we have discussed, that this shift had a deeper and more personal meaning?

Please follow my rationale. At the beginning of the Gospel we are all strangers, searching for meaning. Our relationships with God and with one another are formal at best. However, by the beginning of Acts the informality has been stripped away, and we not only call Jesus Lord, we also call him friend. Maybe the shift in Luke's greetings serves as a metaphor for what all of us have been offered in the good news—namely, friendship with God and a place in God's plan.

Perhaps Luke uses his friend Theophilus as a way of reminding us that this world-transforming narrative, our common story, rests within our care and protection. If true, it helps explain why Luke chose to end his Gospel by focusing on the doubts of the disciples, not on the glory of Jesus' ascent into heaven.

Miracles, Medicines, and Magic

On November 8, 1991, basketball great Ervin "Magic" Johnson disclosed that he had tested positive for HIV. I sat in the parsonage of the small church I pastored, shocked but somewhat relieved. Magic Johnson was the first heterosexual sports figure to disclose his HIV status while at the height of his career. His announcement, though moving and sad, was critical for the HIV community. Overnight, Magic Johnson brought the discussion of HIV/AIDS into the mainstream. Prior to his disclosure, HIV was primarily thought of as a disease that affected homosexuals and drug users. The small percentage of people who contracted the disease through blood transfusions and blood products was considered innocent bystanders. As a result, the public at large had been able to avoid dealing with HIV as an impending crisis for all human beings, not just those whom some labeled as social outcasts. Now everything had changed.

Magic Johnson's announcement spurred increased research-and-development opportunities that brought forth a stream of new medicines and treatments. Prior to 1991, few treatments existed for fighting the disease. The first, approved in 1987, was zidovudine, commonly known as AZT. I began taking AZT in early 1990 as a result of falling CD4 counts. A dropping CD4 count indicates increased damage to the body's immune system. The body's inability to respond to infections is the hallmark of HIV.

My condition was monitored by a local physician who never felt qualified for long-term care and informed me that eventually I would need the supervision of an infectious disease specialist. At the time we were unaware of anyone in my local area who specialized in HIV. Thus, my only option was to see someone in Jackson or New Orleans. After my counts began to drop, finding a specialist became a priority. But I was unprepared for what I would discover.

Referred to the University of Mississippi Medical Center in Jackson, I found the infectious disease department to be an uncomfortable, morose environment. My first visit did not go well. After a long wait, I was put through a battery of tests and examinations by the residents and interns, whose bedside manners were awful, to put it mildly. After being poked and prodded, I left there with my prescription for AZT, feeling more like a science experiment than a patient. As I walked out the door, I informed the infectious disease doctor that I would never return—and I didn't.

For nearly a year I searched for a physician, all the while getting AZT refills and checkups from various local physicians. The primary struggle was to find a doctor not only who was knowledgeable and would be willing to deal with issues of HIV/AIDS, but also to whom I could also relate as a person.

In the summer of 1991, my dentist told me of a doctor in an adjacent town who had been seeing HIV patients for several years. My doctor, Nancy Tatum, a former high school music teacher, worked with her father in a small family-practice clinic. She started seeing HIV patients by accident several years earlier. She had been called into the emergency room at the local hospital to treat one of her former music students who was showing signs of an unusual type of pneumonia. The young man had recently moved home from another state after several months of a prolonged illness. Nancy, my doctor, quickly realized that the illness was AIDS and that the pneumonia was one of the opportunistic infections associated with it. She later told me that, after seeing her former student, she went immediately to the restroom and scrubbed herself from head to toe. Even for medical professionals, the early days of HIV/AIDS were uncertain. Nancy cared for the young man, and it appeared that in so doing she became the first physician in the area to treat people with HIV.

Word spread, clandestinely at first, that Nancy was seeing those infected with this little-known illness. By the time I met her, nearly 150 patients with HIV were being treated in her clinic.

Nancy did not look or act like the stereotypical modern physician. She was more of a throwback to the small-town doctors of the 1940s and 1950s. Her clinic, off of Main Street, was in an older, ranch-style house that smelled of cleaning supplies and alcohol. It seemed straight out of an episode of *Marcus Welby, M.D.*

The first things I noticed about Nancy were her smile and her optimistic attitude. I realized immediately that to her patients she was more than just a doctor; she was also a friend and advocate. My first visit with her was like a long, deep breath, relieving the pent-up pressure caused by months of anxiety and uncertainty. Although an excellent physician, Nancy's greatest gift to her patients was the affirmation of her presence and her willingness to support them in the oftentimes painful, debilitating journey that AIDS represents. A lifelong United Methodist and committed Christian, Nancy felt that her relationship with her patients with HIV was more than just medicine; it was ministry. For me, after months of worrying about what direction to go medically and wondering what twists and turns the next blood count would bring, finding her was nothing short of a miracle.

And yet, even then I could never have imagined how important she would become in my life. In that first year of our doctor-patient relationship, Nancy helped stabilize both my medical and emotional approaches to the disease. She saw me mature as a person living with HIV and showed me how I could help others by sharing my story, albeit privately in those days. My fear of facing the disease head-on was replaced with a quiet determination to fight, and with hope for what tomorrow might bring. One of Nancy's valued services to her patients was to update us continually on the newest medical breakthroughs. Even though for many it would be too late, or the side effects would prevent any real benefit, Nancy turned the news into a reason for celebration. Her favorite saying was, "You are all going to outlive me!"

But Nancy buried too many of her patients over those years, and the strains were taking a toll. Seeing the need to engage and shape the doctors of the future, she decided to go into teaching, taking a teaching position in a local medical school.

The loss of Nancy as a friend and physician coincided with my move to Duke Divinity School. Remarkably, though, Nancy and I stayed in touch. When I returned from Duke, she was busy practicing medicine in Jackson and teaching at the medical school. We quickly resumed our relationship, both as friends and as doctor/patient. As our friendship grew, so did my work in the HIV/AIDS community. What had begun as reluctant participation became part of my ministry.

Nancy's lead in this area had profound effects not only in Mississippi but also throughout the entire Southeast, as she gave her skills, thoughts, and energy in the cause. Working with Nancy changed my life, not just in terms of my own health condition, but in how I saw the world and in how I tried to change my small part of it. Her unwavering optimism and gentle prophecies of a better way kept many, including me, fighting for each day.

Sadly, in 1998, Nancy's favorite saying came true. She had always said that many of her patients would outlive her, and we were shocked when she passed away suddenly. Not quite fifty years old, Nancy discovered a mass at the base of her trachea. The exploratory surgery and tests revealed cancer. After being confronted with the news of this discovery, her friends and family gathered in the recovery room to cheer her up and then left, prepared to support her long fight against the dreaded disease. No one could have known that it was the last time we would see her alive. During the night, she suffered a massive stroke while in intensive care.

The next few days were as difficult as I have ever experienced. The funeral was a blur, and afterward I walked around in a fog, trying to picture my life without this dear friend and supporter. Finally, after nearly a month, I awoke to read a devotional from Mark 1 about Jesus and the leper at the gate. As I read the story, I realized that Nancy, like Jesus, spent her time responding to one forgotten person after another, and that those of us who had known her should dwell not on the loss of Nancy, but on the tremendous gift that her short life afforded us. Along with patience and focus, Nancy's life taught us the hope in seizing the moment and working to make a difference.

One Last Meal

As described by Luke at the beginning of Acts, the risen Jesus gathered the disciples together one last time. This "last supper" was different from the one they shared in the Upper Room prior to his arrest. That first meal had been urgent and serious; this meal was more relaxed as Jesus spoke once again about the kingdom of God and the disciples' place in it.

Jesus said to them, "Do not leave Jerusalem until the Father sends you what he promised." It was not the first time he had talked about the impending arrival of God's spirit. In fact, on two other occasions following the Resurrection, Jesus encouraged the disciples to be vigilant in waiting for this gift.

Spirit and then watching us merely get by. Our place in the family of God makes all of us children and heirs, not lepers sitting at the city gates. We can choose today to take hold of the gift. It is our help, our comfort, and our strength. We are heirs to God's wonderful message of redemption, and it is our golden scepter.

More than anything, though, the gift of the Holy Spirit connects us to the heart of God. Beyond what we can read in any book, it brands our souls and reminds us to whom we belong. Before the Crucifixion, before the Resurrection, Jesus described the gift in words that ring out across the centuries.

> Don't be troubled. You trust God, now trust in me. There are many rooms in my Father's home, and I am going to prepare a place for you. If this were not so, I would tell you plainly. When everything is ready, I will come and get you, so that you will always be with me where I am. And you know where I am going and how to get there. (John 14:1-4 NLT)

Oh, dear friends, brothers, and sisters in faith: The kingdom waits!

First Words Last

I write these final thoughts while sitting in the swing on the front porch of my home. I am amazed at what I see. To my right is a fence, built with my own hands, that runs down the edge of my property. The posts are appropriately placed, if not a little crooked, and the image serves as a nice backdrop to the sloping front yard. The fence took me nearly four weeks to finish.

The front yard is bordered by several flower beds that have become not only a hobby for my wife and me but also an opportunity to retreat from the daily grind of the world. However, they were not built to be either, but were the result of simply not knowing what to do with the various spaces, none of which were considered suitable for much. Funny how unsuitable places can become fertile soil for some of life's most beautiful things.

I walk from the front porch and around the corner of the house. To my left is a stone path I built that connects my front driveway to the backyard. The pavers are flagstone with severe jagged edges. Now firmly placed within the ground, supported by sand and dirt, they look as though they have been there for many years.

The path ends at the base of three red maple trees planted in honor of my children. The trees are gifts from the church I founded and formerly pastored, as a reminder that each of my children was born during my tenure there. Three beautiful gifts—my girls and the trees.

In the backyard are the less notable things of nature and the more noticeable apparatus of our life: the soccer goal, the trampoline, the wooden bridge where Peter Pan saves Wendy, and the fire pit, a favorite place for conversation and, lest we forget, s'mores. Each of these items represents a busy stage of my life that I know will one day fade away but is oh so sweet to endure. In the midst of the grand events of life, they are common reminders that life actually happened while we were busy watching, working, and waiting for other things. In many ways, they are the most important proof that it all means something.

This book has been, at times, a joy; at other times it has been confusing, difficult, and painful. It consumed nearly a year of my life. In that year, we had our third child. I changed jobs. My wife received tenure as an associate professor and traveled thousands of miles to speaking engagements. (She is amazing!) I preached five revivals and spoke many times to various groups about faith and faithfulness. I also buried two pets, built three sections of fence, installed a stone path, two flower beds, a picnic table, a soccer goal, and a trampoline. While I worked to finish this book, life went on and, I might add, quite profoundly. I realize now that going on is all that life knows to do.

Acts 2: Going On

As the door shut behind them, the disciples did not know what to expect. Told to wait for the gift of the Holy Spirit, they gathered with a sense of expectation but also deep uneasiness. Much of their experience with Jesus involved waiting. The patient flow and work of God, which would one day make sense, at this time seemed almost dreadful. Still, they waited and watched for God's next chapter to unfold.

Maybe Peter felt it first. Although knowing that Jesus had ascended, there was a sense of someone other than themselves in the room. However, what their physical senses were telling them did not compare to what their souls were screaming. They looked at one another as the same feeling moved across each of their spirits. Finally Peter tried to say something, but instead of words, the sound came out as a sort of melody.

Individual flames appeared and began to settle on each person in the room. The sound of wind, which earlier had indicated only a small breeze, now echoed a full-blown storm. The room was filled with sights and sounds unseen and unheard.

Others began to speak, but, like Peter, their words came out as melodies. Though foreign to their ears, the words seemed strangely familiar to their hearts, and as they sang, people in the streets began to hear each song in their own language. It was oddly comfortable to hear so many different languages at once—one culture blending with the next, until a chorus of God's Spirit rang through the town. The chorus carried for some time, and then, as the mayhem subsided, Peter addressed the crowd: "Listen carefully, all of you . . ." (Acts 2:14 NLT). And, he proceeded to preach the first of many sermons that detailed the good news of Jesus Christ and to which this new community of faith would devote itself.

Living Life Differently

Recently, the son of a friend won a Grammy Award for cowriting a song entitled "Live Like You Were Dying." The song, which made a huge splash in the country music world, described one man's encounter with a terminal illness that ultimately freed him to live life to the fullest. He learned to live with reckless abandon, squeezing every moment from every day.

Not long after the song was released, it occurred to me that God wants each of us to find such an intimate connection to living, but not simply in the moment. There is a deeper life that God beckons us to try, and, for the few who test it, God unveils the magic of setting aside one's self and discovering the mystery of true relationship. This relationship transforms us and, like the dawn of a new day, possesses all the potential for hope and redemption that faith in God promises. You see, that is what Christ wanted the disciples to understand: that as they began their journey into the world, it was all new, and the sting of yesterday's woes no longer held power. Their tears were finished (Mary), questions answered (the women), fears relinquished (the road to Emmaus), peace discovered (Thomas), purpose assured (the Great Commission), story entrenched (the campfire), and hope secured (promise of the Holy Spirit). This inauspicious band of fishermen, malcontents, marginalized, and forgotten was poised to change the world. Jesus taught them something better than to "live like you were dying"; he taught them to live as those raised from death itself.

A Final Word

Over the next days, months, and years, the community of believers formed in every nook and cranny from Jerusalem to Rome. The apostles and their message spread to every land, and converts from every tribe and nation ignited this movement of the Way into a potent force that eventually altered human history—sometimes manifesting itself in ways that were very different from the original intention, but always being *sent*. I believe that Craig Van Gelder, in his book *The Essence of the Church* (Grand Rapids: Baker Books, 2000), says it best: "The church is more than what meets the eye. It is more than a set of well-managed ministry functions. It is more than another human organization. The church lives in the world as a human enterprise, but (ultimately) it is the called and redeemed people of God" (pp. 24-25).

The church is also our grand point of reference, reminding us of our true spiritual heritage that was forged in places such as Golgotha, Galilee, and Bethany, forged against the backdrops of personal encounters in real places by very real people. It is that gentle, resounding echo that enables every Christian who listens for the whisper of God's word to find what we seek, to see what we should not believe, and to hear the waves crashing at the Sea of Galilee and the voice of one standing on the shore still calling, "Follow me."

STUDY GUIDE

This study guide provides additional focus for individuals and small groups interested in developing their understanding of the *seven next words*. Written to encourage dialogue and reflection, each section is divided into four parts.

The first part, *Reveal*, allows for a deeper unveiling of the scripture text. Although certainly not exhaustive in nature, the questions provide a starting point for further discussion. The second part, *Reflect*, addresses more personal questions derived from themes of the texts by encouraging readers to think diligently about how the text affects, instructs, and ignites their particular perspective on the topic. The third section, *Respond*, enlists the readers to transform words into action by responding to the words of Christ in tangible ways that can have an effect on their world. The last section, *Refine*, takes the readers deeper into scripture and self-discovery by addressing various supplemental texts and principles in each of the seven encounters.

One suggestion is to use the study guide during the seven weeks of Eastertide (the seven Sundays including and following Easter Sunday). Each week represents a particular focus that allows the reader to participate fully in the post-Resurrection texts.

The purpose of these questions is to immerse seekers and believers in the wonderful, powerful, and poignant story of those important days following Jesus' resurrection. And, so, to that end, may God richly bless and guide us.

THE FIRST WORD

Who are you looking for?

Read the scripture: John 20:1-18

REVEAL

1. Discuss the reactions of Peter, John, and Mary at the tomb. How are they different? Why are these differing reactions and perspectives important?

2. Discuss why the writer of the Gospel places so much emphasis on the physical description of where Jesus' body had been. How do these descriptions relate to Mary's inability to recognize the risen Jesus?

3. Discuss Mary's response to Jesus in verse 15. Why would Mary mistake Jesus for the gardener? What words would you use to describe Mary's state of mind?

4. Why does Jesus, in verse 17, instruct Mary not to "hold on to me"?

REFLECT

1. Had you been at the tomb on Easter morning, would you have been a Peter, a John, or a Mary? What characteristics of this character do you recognize in yourself?

2. In what ways have you missed the risen Jesus in your daily walk? What circumstances prevent you from seeing or recognizing him?

3. How would you finish this statement? "Today, I am looking for . . ."

RESPOND

1. What spiritual habits or disciplines should you begin to or further develop in order to encounter Jesus in your world?

2. What broken or dying relationships in your life need forgiveness and restoration? How can you begin the healing process?

REFINE

1. Read Luke 10:38-42. Describe what Martha and Mary, respectively, are looking for. How are their individual needs different?

2. Describe Jesus' response to Martha. Do you believe Jesus' response is harsh?

3. Are you more like Martha or Mary in your approach to spiritual matters?

THE SECOND WORD

Greetings . . . Don't be afraid

Read the scripture: Matthew 28:8-10

REVEAL

1. In this, the shortest of the encounters, Jesus meets the women as they go to tell the disciples what they have seen at the tomb. Why, in this encounter, do you think Jesus meets them on the journey instead of at the tomb?
2. The text states that the women were both frightened and joyful. Describe each emotion the women felt, and relate it to other emotions described in the Bible.
3. Discuss Jesus' threefold interaction with the women: (1) greeting, (2) comfort, and (3) task.

REFLECT

1. Has there ever been a time when you were frightened but also excited about a situation? Discuss.
2. Have you ever met Jesus in your daily walk and failed to acknowledge him? How did it affect your spiritual walk?
3. Have you ever met Jesus in your daily walk and succeeded in acknowledging him? How did it affect you?

RESPOND

Today, make plans to respond the way Christ did:
1. Greet a stranger.
2. Provide a word or act of comfort to someone in need.
3. Share a task or assist with one for the betterment of someone else.

REFINE

1. Frank refers to a passage of scripture that was read at his wife's funeral service describing four ways in which God addresses our fears. Read Proverbs 3:5-6. What are the four ways, and how have they affected your life?

2. Discuss the following quotation from C. S. Lewis: "No one ever told me that grief felt so like fear. I am not afraid, but the sensation is like being afraid. The same fluttering in the stomach, the same restlessness, the yawning. I keep on swallowing" (chap. 1 in *A Grief Observed*). Now contrast that quotation with the following statement: God often uses our most difficult moments to show us the sweetest glimpses of faith and joy.

THE THIRD WORD

What are you so concerned about?

Read the scripture: Luke 24:13-34

REVEAL

1. What would have been some topics of conversation between the two men as they walked the road to Emmaus (v. 14)?
2. Why do you believe God withheld Jesus' identity from the two men (v. 16)?
3. Given the topics discussed by the two men, who do you think they were? What might have been their vocations and their cultural standing (vv. 17-20)?
4. Discuss the phrase "we had thought he was the Messiah" (v. 21).
5. Jesus responded with an assertive tone in verses 25-26. What do you believe was Jesus' intention in doing so?
6. How did the meal that the men shared with Jesus affect their understanding of the situation, and why (vv. 30-32)?

REFLECT

1. Describe a time when you missed seeing the work of God in your midst.
2. Discuss the importance of the "table" in our spiritual journeys. How does Holy Communion model God's intentions for helping the family of believers recognize Jesus?

RESPOND

1. Plan a special meal for spiritual friends and seekers. This may include friends, family, coworkers, and others who have been far from God or who are experiencing a difficult situation.
2. Create a "walking with Jesus" journal in which you document the ways you see God working in the world.

REFINE

1. Read John 16:33. Jesus makes two "promises" to us about the future. What are they, and how do they address our present-day fears and uncertainties?
2. During Jake's final days, he kept a journal in which he listed five scriptures that show how God eases our concerns in this world. Please read the following scripture texts and list the ways in which they show God respond to our needs.
   Galatians 3:21-29
   John 14:15-18
   John 14:16
   Romans 8:28
   Hebrews 6:18

THE FOURTH WORD

Peace be with you

Read the scripture: Luke 24:35-43; John 20:19-29

REVEAL

1. Review the story of the walk to Emmaus (Luke 24:13-34). Referring to the current scripture text, what was now different from what Jesus first encountered from the two men on the road to Emmaus?
2. Why does Jesus ask the disciples to look at his hands and feet to counter their unbelief?
3. Why does Jesus ask for something to eat?

REFLECT

1. Describe several ways that God speaks in our world today. What is the primary means by which God gets your attention?
2. What causes you to doubt? How does doubt affect our walk with God (positively and negatively)?
3. Describe the spiritual disciplines you currently use in your daily journey. How could they be deepened or refined for use in the world?

RESPOND

1. Make an effort to deepen your spiritual disciplines. Try journaling or participating in a covenant group, prayer group, or small group Bible study to model the peace-full life of Jesus.
2. How can you be a peacemaker in your community? Are there individuals in your life to whom you should offer or show peace today?
3. What are your greatest impediments to a peace-full life (hurry, apathy, discontentment, and so on)?

REFINE

1. Read Galatians 5:17-21. What does Paul say about the self-sufficient life? List and discuss at least five attributes.
2. Now, read verses 22-26. What does the faith-full life provide? Name and discuss at least four things.

THE FIFTH WORD

Go into the world

Read the scripture: Matthew 28:18-20; Mark 16:15-18; Luke 24:45-49

REVEAL

1. Describe the similarities and differences between the various Great Commission texts.
2. What do you believe Jesus means by "all the world" or "all nations"?
3. Describe the importance of the disciples' "doubt" and "struggle" just prior to each Great Commission text.

4. What principles are the disciples encouraged to share in order to "make disciples" of all people?

REFLECT

1. Which Great Commission theme or text most relates to your personal spiritual journey?
2. Describe some ways you can "go" into your world today. What prevents you from witnessing to the good news? How does your personal spiritual journey affect your ability to witness?

RESPOND

1. Design, lead, or attend an outreach ministry for seekers in your community or church.
2. Make a list of family or friends who need your prayer, support, and encouragement in their spiritual walk. In what specific ways can you respond to their needs?

REFINE

1. Read Romans 10:13-15. What is the importance of hearing God's word?
2. According to the chapter, what three things must we do to hear God's word? Discuss your reactions to the three.
3. What are the four predominant themes of each Great Commission text, and how do you respond to each?

THE SIXTH WORD

Have you caught any fish?

Read the scripture: John 21:1-23

REVEAL

1. Read Luke 5:1-11. Describe the similarities and differences between the two "Great Catch" texts. Why do you believe the texts are so similar, yet occur at different points in Jesus' ministry on earth?

2. What is the significance of Jesus' gathering the disciples around the campfire? Discuss the possible conversation topics.
3. Why do you think John (the writer of the text) felt the need to count the number of fish caught?
4. Discuss the phrase "and no one dare ask him if he really was the Lord because they were sure of it."
5. Discuss Jesus' interaction with Peter. Why does Jesus ask Peter the question three times? What do you believe Jesus means in asking Peter to "feed my sheep"?
6. Describe Peter's comments concerning the apostle John's future.

REFLECT

1. Describe a special meal or holiday gathering in your life. Why does this memory remain so important to you?
2. What circumstances in your life either support or inhibit your following Jesus?
3. Describe a time when envy or jealousy prevented you from doing or living out God's will in your life.

RESPOND

1. Invite someone who might need encouragement to lunch or for coffee or soda. What are some other ways you can encourage him or her in the journey?
2. Make a list of God's sheep whom you can feed today.

REFINE

1. Read Mark 5:21-43. How does this pre-Resurrection encounter of Jesus fit within the "common story" of faith as an example of what Jesus would call the disciples to do?
2. What is Jairus's concern before Jesus? How does Jesus respond to his request?
3. Discuss the woman's condition. Why are her actions so incredible for people to behold?
4. When people tell Jairus not to bother Jesus any longer, how does Jesus respond?

5. Describe the significance of the number twelve in both scenes.
6. Read Hebrews 11. How does the "Great Story of Faith" compare with your story of faith?

THE SEVENTH WORD

Wait for the gift

Read the scripture: Acts 1:1-11

REVEAL

1. Discuss the importance, connection, and focus of Luke's two New Testament books (the Gospel of Luke and the book of Acts).
2. What is the significance of the number forty in the text (v. 3)? Where else does the number appear in scripture, and why is that important?
3. Why does Jesus instruct the disciples not to leave Jerusalem? Why would he refer to John the Baptist in this final moment?
4. What is the significance for the disciples of "restoring the kingdom of Israel"?
5. What is the gift of the Holy Spirit? How will this gift affect the disciples' future?
6. Why do the "white-robed men" question the disciples about looking into the sky?

REFLECT

1. Name the best gift you have ever received. Why was it so special?
2. Have you ever missed the point when God was trying to reveal something new to you? Describe and discuss.
3. Have you ever taken a spiritual gift assessment? If yes, when and what was your gift? If no, what do you believe is your spiritual gift?
4. Where and with whom do you feel most comfortable sharing your faith journey?

RESPOND

1. If you haven't already done so, take some steps toward discovering your area of passion in ministry. How do your spiritual gifts inform your response to God's call on your life?

2. Be deliberate in spending more time in devotion, service, and witness of your faith. How and where can God use you today?

REFINE

1. Describe the literal and figurative significance of Theophilus in the Gospel of Luke and the book of Acts.
2. At the Ascension, Jesus instructs the disciples to focus on three principles. What are they, and how do they relate to our lives today?
3. Read Mark 1:41-45. What did the leper ask of Jesus? How did Jesus respond? Discuss your reactions to both. How does "willingness" affect our ministry's impact?

WORKS CITED

Isaacson, Walter. *Benjamin Franklin: An American Life.* New York: Simon & Schuster, 2003.

Lewis, C. S. *A Grief Observed.* San Francisco: HarperSanFrancisco, 1961.

Nouwen, Henri J. M. *Reaching Out: The Three Movements of the Spiritual Life.* Garden City, N.Y.: ImageBooks, 1986.

Petersen, Eugene. *The Message: The Bible in Contemporary Language.* Colorado Springs: NavPress Publishing Group, 1993.

Stanford, Shane, and Ronnie Kent. *Salt and Light: Twenty-five Days for Making Life Matter.* Longwood, Fla.: Xulon Press, 2003.

Van Gelder, Craig. *The Essence of the Church: A Community Created by the Spirit.* Grand Rapids: Baker Books, 2000.

ACKNOWLEDGMENTS

How do you begin to say *thank you* to anyone and everyone who has helped in developing a project like this? Of all that I have written over the last months, this section has taken the longest. I know any author desires to make sure that no one is left out or forgotten—from family members to friends to colleagues who helped shape the design and fabric of the work. There are so many who have encouraged and guided along the way. The following could not possibly include everyone who has made what you experienced in the previous pages possible. But, here it goes, a few thank-you's for those who have made it all so meaningful.

To Bishop Ken Carder, for your gentle encouragement and support.

To Kurt, the finest, most irreverent traveling buddy anyone could ask for, for keeping me from taking myself too seriously.

To *The Group*—Grif, for your practical assistance and faithful friendship; Jimmy, for your badgering, mixed with unbelievable prayers and support; Ronnie, for your continued wisdom, care, and guidance, not only as a friend, but as my hero and mentor; and Robert, for your constant encouragement and for showing me the best example of a friend anyone could ever know.

To Jeff, an amazing friend and project partner—so many tractors, so little time . . .

To Mike, a great friend and even better physician, for your expertise and commitment to my health, sometimes in spite of me.

To Shannon, Lisa, and Randa, for encouraging me to stay focused on the really important things in life.

To Patty and Nanny, for your incredible sense of possibilities, even when I couldn't see them. Thank you for your critique and care.

To Jason, for your continued support through the years and for being the source of some of my best illustrations. Your friendship is one of my life's most enduring treasures.

To Dad, for your gift of the written and spoken word and for the encouragement to make it my own.

Acknowledgments

To Buford, for always being willing to drop everything and go. You're the best disciple maker I know.

To Whitney, for your fire, faith, and friendship. You would make any big brother very proud.

To Mom, still the best witness and disciple I have ever known. Thank you for teaching me never to give up and never forget for Whom it matters.

To Sarai Grace, Juli Anna, and Emma Leigh, for reminding me that the most important work I do on this side of heaven requires pink, lace, and ponytails. You are more than my children; you are my inspiration.

To Pokey, for the gift of your love, support, and friendship, and for the gift of your heart on that hot August day. But, more than anything, thank you for the three most precious treasures that any father could ask for. I love you.

And to Jesus, our Dearest Friend. Thank you, above all, for continuing to whisper those sweet *next* words into my soul, even when I didn't want to hear them. Until that day, I will go where you send.

> John, meanwhile, had been locked up in prison. When he got wind of what Jesus was doing, he sent his own disciples to ask, "Are you the One we've been expecting, or are we still waiting?" Jesus told them, "Go back and tell John what's going on: The blind see, The lame walk, Lepers are cleansed, The deaf hear, The dead are raised, The wretched of the earth learn that God is on their side.
>
> Matthew 11:2-5 (Message)